HIP-HOP PRODUCTION
INSIDE THE BEATS

PRINCE CHARLES ALEXANDER

This book is dedicated to my dear mother, Marie Nelda (neé Gautier) Alexander (1931 to 2008)
who always told me the truth, even unto its innermost parts.
I love you forever!

And to my beautiful wife Candice Christine (neé Coggins) Alexander.
I love you always!

BERKLEE PRESS
Editor in Chief: Jonathan Feist
Senior Vice President of Online Learning and Continuing Education/CEO of Berklee Online: Debbie Cavalier
Vice President of Enrollment Marketing and Management: Mike King
Vice President of Academic Strategy: Carin Nuernberg
Editorial Assistants: Emily Jones, Brittany McCorriston, Megan Richardson
Production Exercise Assistants: Ariel Rodriguez, Brian Walker
Illustrator: Alice Lee

ISBN 978-0-87639-211-9

Berklee Press

1140 Boylston Street
Boston, MA 02215-3693 USA
(617) 747-2146

Visit Berklee Press Online at
www.berkleepress.com

Berklee Online

Study music online at
online.berklee.edu

Distributed By

HAL•LEONARD®
—A Muse Group Company—

Visit Hal Leonard Online
www.halleonard.com

Berklee Press, a publishing activity of Berklee College of Music, is a not-for-profit educational publisher.
Available proceeds from the sales of our products are contributed to the scholarship funds of the college.

CONTENTS

ACKNOWLEDGMENTS

The Family: Adella "Adella, Adella, the Storyteller" Gautier (RIP), Tiffany Chase, Amber Zu-Bolton, Troy Sears Lewis, Leslie Sears-Barone, Vernon Sears, Tessie Shanahan, Albert Sears, Sydney Dailey, and my extended family descended from Julia Watson Dailey Gautier Lee (affectionately known as Mama); Annie "Mom" Talbert, Sheila Talbert, Joel Talbert, Bunny Talbert, Larry Talbert (RIP), Pam Talbert, and Michael Talbert; Candice Alexander, Chloe Alexander, and Aden Alexander; Romeo Alexander PhD, Catherine Wideman, and John Wideman; Katrina Jackson, Big Rico Jackson, and Eileen Hollis; Khemis Jackson, Kailynn Jackson, Karon Jackson, and Baby Rico Jackson; Louis Alfred, Stephen Alfred, Bruce Purse, and Theresa Griffith.

Production Exercise Assistants: Ariel Rodriguez, Brian Walker.

The Muses: Roscoe Gorham, José Ramos, Charles "Chucky" Snow, John Carrington, Rev. Miniard Culpepper, Larry "Maurice Starr" Johnson, Conant "Tony" Rose, Marilyn and Marlene Muldrow, CL "Dr. Funkenchain" Kelly, James and Lynette Johnson, Mark Ledford, Victor Bailey, the City Beat Band (Boston), Ruth Winley, Kim Davis, Greg Barrett, Darryll Mull, Tomas Doncker, Alix Anthony, the City Beat Band (New York), Paul Laurence, Michael "Kashif" Jones, Bruce Purse, Vincent Henry, Vincent McClean, William "Spaceman" Patterson, Melvin Van Peebles, August "Kid Creole" Darnell, Andy "Coati Mundi" Hernandez, Kid Creole and the Coconuts, Les Rita Mitsouko, Bobby Nathan, Joanne Georgio Nathan, Chad "Dr. Ceuss" Elliott, Devante "Swing" Degrate, Jodeci, Dwight "Heavy D" Myers, Usher Raymond, Destiny's Child, Sean "Puff Daddy" Combs, Steven Dent, Mary J. Blige, Christopher "The Notorious B.I.G." Wallace, Faith Evan, Rufus "Blaq" Moore, David "Roz" Rosner, Lou Gonzalez, Carla (Cifarelli) Springer, Doug E. Fresh, Chris Rock, X-Clan, Yolanda "Yo-Yo" Whitaker, Aaron Hall, David "Redhead Kingpin" Guppy, Angie Stone, Luther Vandross, Joe Thomas p/k/a "Joe," Maxi Priest, Cheryl "Salt" James, Stokley Williams, Mint Condition, Lance Alexander, Lo Key?, Alicia Keys, Jennifer Lopez, Mason "Mase" Betha, Total, 112, Carl Thomas, the Lox, Kimberly "Lil Kim" Jones, Horace Brown, Robert "Black Rob" Ross, Trevell "G-Dep" Coleman, Philippe "Akhenaton" Fragioné, Geoffroy "Shurik'n" Mussard, Éric "Khéops" Mazel, Pascal "Imhotep" Perez, François "Kephren" Mendy, IAM, Alliance Ethnik, Abdoulaye "Oxmo Puccino" Diarra, Alliance Ethnik, Femi Kuti, Jimmy Cliff, Frederick "Toots" Hibbert, Toshinori Yonekura, Luca Minchillo, Nalini, Spearhead, Youssou N'Dour, Gordon Chambers, Donny McClurkin, Troy Germano, Kurtis "Blow" Walker, Hank Shocklee, Grandmaster Flash, Remy Fisher, Dr. Scot Brown, Ohene Savant, Elai Tubo.

Thanks also to Carl Beatty, Rob Jaczko, Dan Thompson, and Jason Stokes at Berklee College of Music; Nick Sansano at the NYU Clive Davis Institute of Recorded Music; the Recording Academy P&E Wing; and the Audio Engineering Society (AES).

INTRODUCTION

Hip-hop is an innovative and rebellious art form credited with birth in the Sedgwick Housing Projects, Bronx, NY, on August 11, 1973. DJ Kool Herc is the party thrower that turned playing recorded music (on two turntables instead of one) into a skill that changed American music listening and, soon after, music making. Hip-hop lives on the cutting edge of popular culture, for sure, but it also lies on the bleeding edge of music technology.

Imagine that you are a young DJ Kool Herc—a twenty-something in the Bronx, New York, in the mid 1970s. You own a turntable just like other people in your neighborhood. You give block parties and play the hot jams of the day, just like other DJs in your neighborhood. And something inside you tells you that if you had *two* turntables and a mixer, you could alternate a beat between the two turntables and extend a four-bar musical pattern—you know, that hot break section in the middle of that fly record—you could extend that musical pattern to infinity.

What a brilliant idea. Nobody had done this before. No one had heard this before. Where did this spirit of musical/technical innovation come from? Was it divine providence, boredom, or an accident? Or was it a byproduct of youthful rebellion against entrenched concepts? A youthful rebellion that perpetually infuses soul into art, soul into culture, and yes—dare I say it, dare I put the two words together—soul into technology?

Extending sections of records assaults the senses of the norm and is challenged almost immediately as an appropriative art form, lacking in its own ability to conceive harmony, melody, and rhythm. "You're just playing someone else's record." True, but didn't Andy Warhol just paint a picture of someone else's soup can? The DJ uses the turntable as his canvas full of prerecorded pictures waiting for a collage of invention.

As a musician, at the time, I thought for sure this was an uneducated use of recorded music and a major violation of copyright laws. But in retrospect, when has any new, self-respecting art form bowed down to constraints? Spirituals, blues, Dixieland, jazz, swing, big band, rhythm and blues, doo-wop, rock 'n' roll, soul, funk, and disco all created heated debates in their time—just like the debate that Kool Herc, that kid from the Bronx, created in the mid 1970s.

Copyright law was definitely a stumbling block, however. The first commercially successful rap record ("Rapper's Delight" by the Sugarhill Gang) did not use turntable technology as its musical bed. In an effort to capitalize on the growing street phenomenon called "rap," Sylvia Robinson, a singer who had a successful record in 1973 called *Pillow Talk*, reinvented herself as a record executive and cofounder of

Sugar Hill Records. Sylvia (born in 1936) and her husband, Joe Robinson, figured out a way to mother and nurture this brand-new art form by hiring a live band to play music instead of hiring a DJ to play records behind the Sugarhill Gang. The copyright crisis was averted, questionably, and for a brief time, but hip-hop as a global phenomenon was off to the races.

ABOUT THIS BOOK

This book is intended to focus on the *production of recorded hip-hop music,* so we will trace a timeline that that includes commercially successful hip-hop records and the innovations they showcased.

The art form has definitely influenced pop music; changed how vocalists approach singing, songwriting, and vocal production; and turned into a global art form that has touched every country.

For a job well done, Hip-Hop, you are to be commended. Not only because you have defined DJ'ing/beat making, MC'ing/rapping, breakdancing, and graffiti as the four cornerstones of the hip-hop ecosystem, but because you have gone beyond predictions that you were just a fad of novelty recordings—a "non-music" that appealed to a musically illiterate sensibility. You have done a great job at presenting your case as the latest in a line of genuine American folk music styles.

There are many books written about the culture and sociology of hip-hop, but we will look at the craft of *making hip-hop records,* which is ultimately how hip-hop made its trek across the globe.

If you have beat making skills, take a look at how the *DAW* (Digital Audio Workstation) of your choice can be used to analyze and recreate the concepts from the songs I discuss.

And for all the musicians reading this book that play conventional instruments, please keep this thought in mind: *"Before we can get to the hearts and minds of the music audience, we must first conquer the music itself."*

Prince Charles Alexander

ABOUT THE ONLINE AUDIO

To access the accompanying audio, go to www.halleonard.com/mylibrary and enter the code found on the first page of this book. This will grant you instant access to every example. Examples with accompanying audio are marked with an audio icon. Tracks to be loaded into your DAW for production exercises are indicated by a Download icon.

Audio Download

PART I

Hip-Hop Tools of Production

Making a hip-hop recording takes a certain know-how, and a facility with specific technologies. This section outlines how hip-hop's tools of production helped to define the early stages of its development as a recording art.

CHAPTER 1

The Recording Studio Model and the First Successful Hip-Hop Records: 1979 to 1981

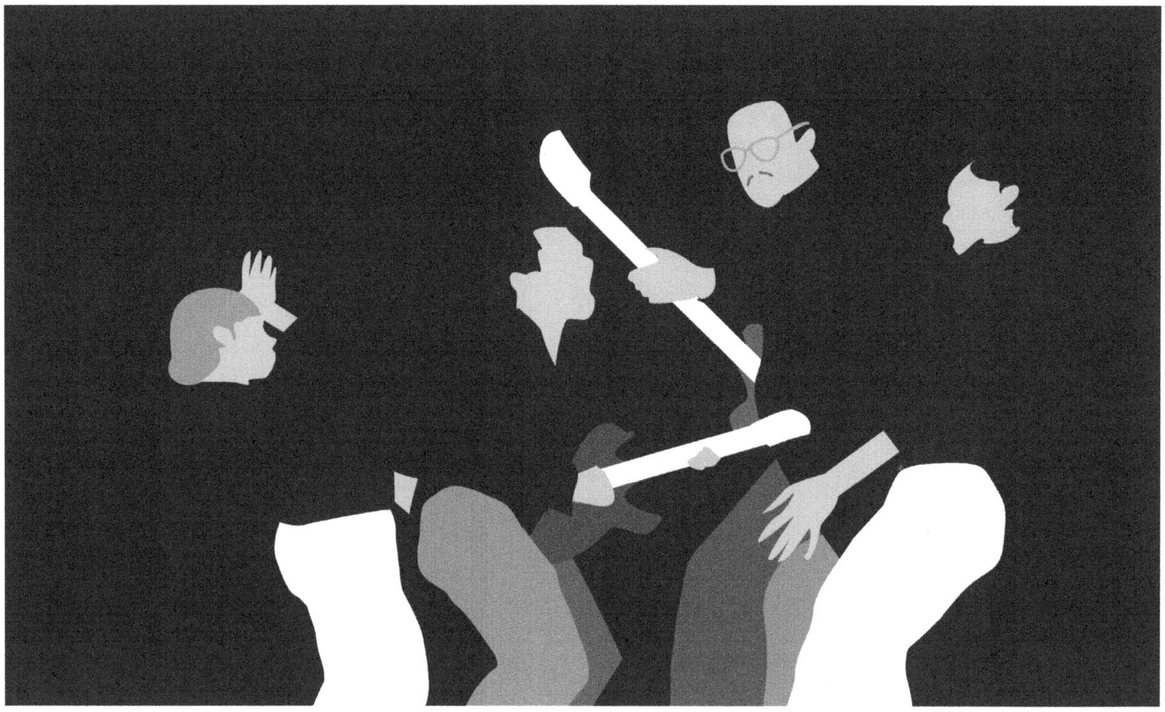

LISTENING: EARLY HIP-HOP

- "Good Times" by Chic (1979)
- "Rapper's Delight" by the Sugarhill Gang (1979)
- "The Breaks" by Kurtis Blow (1980)

The conventional model of recording music—the *live band model*—is the first production model in our hip-hop music production timeline and is responsible for unveiling rap to the rest of the planet. Let's face it, a young black DJ was not going to be playing turntables on American Bandstand in 1979, and you can only play for a limited number of people at block parties using turntables. But once you create a sound recording, the whole world is your available audience.

Drums, bass, guitar, piano, horns, strings, percussion, and vocals recorded in a studio facility using transducers, routers, modifiers, and storage mediums have been approached in a consistent manner to make records since the mid-1950s beginnings of the rock 'n' roll era. Sylvia Robinson preferred this tried-and-true recording method to jump into her exploration of rapping and beat making.

LIVE BANDS IN EARLY HIP-HOP RECORDING

Sylvia Robinson was a former recording artist who hired musicians to replay music for her fledgling record company, Sugar Hill Records. She found rappers who could add their flavor to a sound that people had been talking about for a few years in the New York/New Jersey corridor. Her live-band solution to copyright infringement, however, temporarily robbed hip-hop of one of its major unique components: the turntable.

Many of us thought that the actual recording of Chic's "Good Times" (1979) was the musical bed for "Rapper's Delight." In reality, it was a replayed interpolation of Chic's "Good Times" by a bass player, guitarist, keyboard player, drummer, and percussionist, all recruited by Sylvia Robinson's eighteen-year-old son, Joey Robinson, Jr.

At the time, many thought that "Rapper's Delight" was a fluke—a novelty record, like "Monster Mash" (1962) or "Convoy" (1975), which also featured spoken-word vocals. This was dispelled, however, by the contemporaneous rapid successes of Kurtis Blow's compositions "Christmas Rappin'" (1979) and "The Breaks" (1980), which were also live band productions with rapping, and also huge hits at the time. These breakthrough hits proved that "Rapper's Delight" was not a musical fluke, and that the standard for instrumentation within the young art form had been set.

Also in 1979:

- June, I released my first commercial recording, "In the Streets" by Prince Charles and the City Beat Band.
- August, Nile Rodgers and Bernard Edwards released "Good Times" by their group Chic.
- October, Sylvia and Joe Robinson released "Rapper's Delight" by the Sugarhill Gang.

They were, in order: a funk record, a hybrid disco/soul record, and a rap record. What these recordings had in common is that all were recorded in studios using live bands.

For the record, hip-hop's official birth is credited to DJ Kool Herc in 1973, and expanded due to the "hands-on" innovations of Marley Marl and Grandmaster Flash, but for most of the country, the first commercially successful hip-hop *recording* is credited to "Rapper's Delight" in 1979.

FIG. 1.1. The Sugarhill Gang

By using the most popular dance groove of the period, "Good Times," as the backdrop for the rap verses of "Rapper's Delight," Sylvia's Robinson's Sugar Hill Records production was ready to connect to the dance club scene of the late 1970s and the youth market. Three rappers were chosen—Wonder Mike (Michael Anthony Wright), Master Gee (Guy O'Brien), and Big Bank Hank (Henry Lee Jackson)—to perform their rhymes on top of the "Good Times" cover.

The band that covered the original "Good Times" recording was recreating the DJ'ing technique of extending the break section of a record. The break section was the section, or sections, of a record most focused on drums and percussion only, with minimal to no accompaniment from the other instrumentation. The DJ would then switch playback, back and forth, between two copies of the same record, on two turntables, using a turntable mixer. As one of the records was playing the break, the other record would be backed up to the beginning of that same break. When the first record completed the break section, the fader on the mixer would switch to the second record, and that record would then play the musical break. This could be repeated over and over to extend a musical break for as long as the DJ wanted.

A band, by contrast, could repeat a section of a song by using musicians performing the same section over and over.

Both the live band and the two-turntables-with-mixer approaches were able to extend an existing song, but as of October 1979, no recording had gained national attention extending another artist's existing song by either means.

THE TECHNOLOGY OF LIVE BAND PRODUCTION

The technology used to record the band for "Rapper's Delight" was state-of-the-art for the time. Vocals, drums, percussion, and pianos were recorded using microphones passing through microphone preamps, while electric guitars and electric basses were recorded using amplifiers passing through microphone preamps and/or DI (direct input) boxes passing through line-level amplifiers. All the recorded signals were routed via a recording console to magnetic tape, where they could be stored for playback. This recording path had become the most common way to make contemporary records and had its roots in the first multitrack recordings attempted by Les Paul in the 1950s.

Multitracking is the process where one musician can listen to their recorded performance while simultaneously adding another recorded performance on a separate recording track. The performer can repeat this process again and again, and is only limited by the number of tracks available on their recording machine. The recorded tracks can then be blended (mixed) differently to raise or lower certain instruments. Recorded drums, for instance, got louder and louder in records throughout the 1960s.

Prior to the innovation of multitracking, musicians had to perform as a full ensemble directly to a disc that would later be mass-produced for the listening audience. The rhythm of the older, *live-to-disc*, type of recording was infused with the imperfect, human feel of the drummer and/or percussionists, and the level of loudness for the musicians came from positioning each player at varying distances from the main microphone(s).

Early mass-produced records played back in mono (using only one speaker or headphone), but by the late 1950s and early 1960s, stereo listening (using two speakers or headphones) had become the most popular way to listen to music. Hip-hop used all the technological audio advances that occurred prior to 1979 and eagerly adopted those technological advances that occurred after.

Let's look a bit more at those early technological audio discoveries.

We can begin with the concept of recording. Recordings of acoustic events are artificial, analogous versions of those acoustic events. Playing back recorded sounds does not reproduce those sounds exactly as we hear them, but rather approximates—as well as our equipment can capture and reproduce—the acoustic events that are introduced into the recording medium. The sounds in our recordings are a captured version of sound waves that move through air. As the sound waves pass from the source, through the air of an acoustic space, into the recording path, the recording process turns these acoustic sound waves into electrical energy that can be stored and retrieved at later points in time. The playback process reverses this path by converting the electrical energy back into acoustic sound delivered through the air of our listening space to our ears and brains.

Early hip-hop producers and DJs were playing back audio that had already been recorded, and were turning the playback itself into a creative process by using two turntables and a mixer to extend beats. Later, they were putting their hands on the vinyl playback disc to create new tones, pitches, and rhythms with the existing work. Additionally, though, in order to expand hip-hop's reach, the tried-and-true concept of multitrack recording a live band was used for "Rapper's Delight."

These are the six steps of multitrack recording:

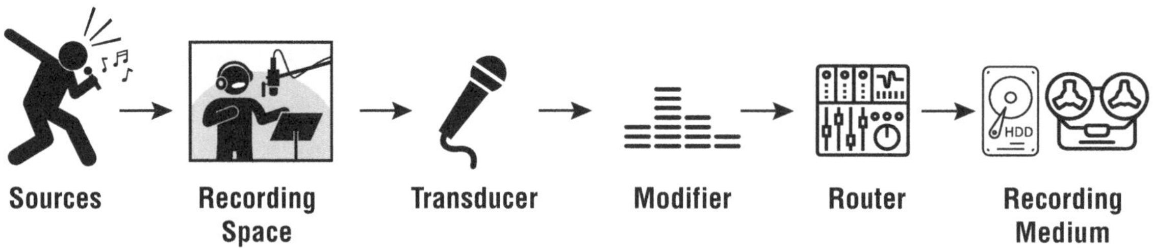

FIG. 1.2. Six Steps of Multitrack Recording

sources:	voices and instruments
recording space:	the rooms where you are recording
transducer:	converts acoustic sounds into electricity (microphones, DI boxes, etc.)
modifier:	alters incoming audio signals (equalizer, compressor, etc.)
router:	moves audio from one point to another (sends and busses)
recording medium:	used to store multiple paths of audio for future retrieval (in 1979, that would be an analog tape machine; digital audio is stored on hard drives)

These are the six steps of audio playback:

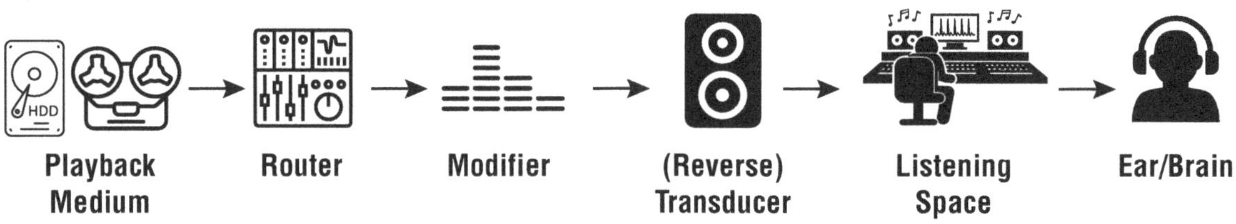

FIG. 1.3. Six Steps of Audio Playback

playback medium:	used to retrieve stored audio for playback (tape machine or hard drive)
router:	moves audio to the output points in the playback system
modifier:	alters outgoing audio signals (equalizer, compressor, reverb/delay)
(reverse) transducer:	converts electrical energy into acoustic energy (a loudspeaker, also known as an audio monitor)
listening space:	the rooms wherein you critically listen to audio playback
ear/brain:	how music is perceived and enjoyed

TRANSDUCERS

The mechanical journey of hip-hop performances begins and is eventually enjoyed by the consumer because of the conversion properties of transducers. Transducers convert acoustic energy to electrical energy or electrical energy to acoustic energy. Microphones, speakers, and headphones, an important part of how hip-hop traversed the planet, are all transducers.

Microphones

Microphone selection is where producers and engineers begin the process of record production. Choosing microphones well and listening to speakers correctly can make or break a production, hip-hop or otherwise.

There are different types of transducer constructions and operations used in microphones, and other transducers. The dynamic, ribbon, condenser, piezo, carbon, and crystal methods are some of the different families of transducers. The two types that are the most common in hip-hop are the condenser and the dynamic.

Condenser Microphones

Condenser microphones are the microphones of choice in studio recording situations. Their response to a wide range of audio frequencies is superior to the response characteristics of most other microphone designs, thus making them the perfect tool for flexible instruments such as the human voice. This design usually requires a power source, provided either from microphone inputs as phantom power or from a small internal battery. Power is needed to conduct the capacitor plate voltage that moves the diaphragm in response to incoming audio signals. Since the output of this type of microphone is usually low, power is also necessary for internal amplification of the signal to a useful output level. When two diaphragms are used in a condenser design (dual-diaphragm), they can provide the unidirectional, bidirectional, and omnidirectional microphone patterns that sound engineers use to capture audio. Although considered more fragile than their sturdier counterparts, some of the most expensive and highest quality microphones are condensers.

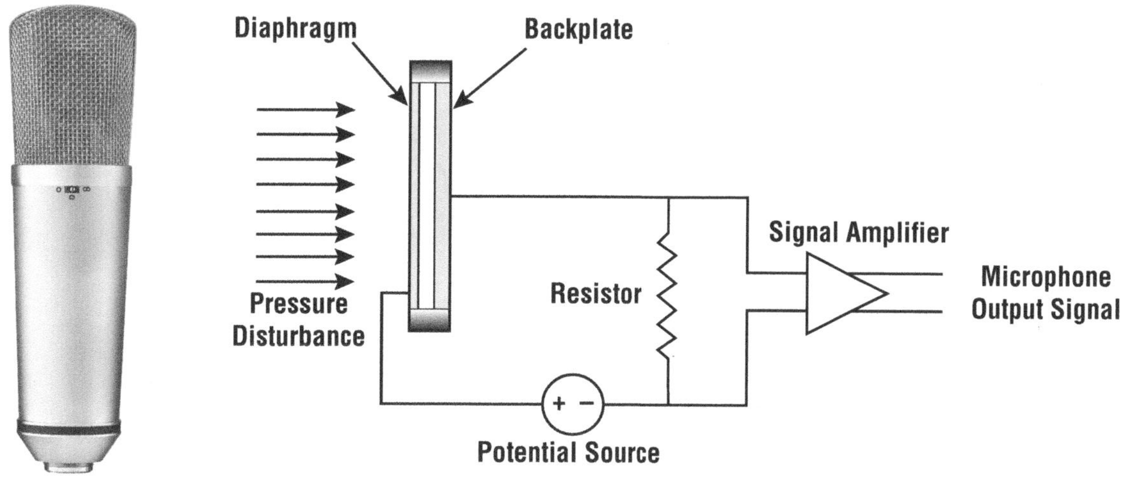

FIG. 1.4. Condenser Microphone Cross-Section

Dynamic Microphones

Dynamic microphones are based on the principle of electromagnetic induction. A coil is wound around a magnet, and it moves in response to pressure from audio sources that act on an attached diaphragm. These microphones are relatively inexpensive, sturdy, and can handle the outdoor elements well. They are commonly used in live applications but are also a staple of a well-rounded studio collection. This design is also called the moving coil and has a close cousin called the ribbon microphone that uses a thin strip of aluminum instead of a copper coil.

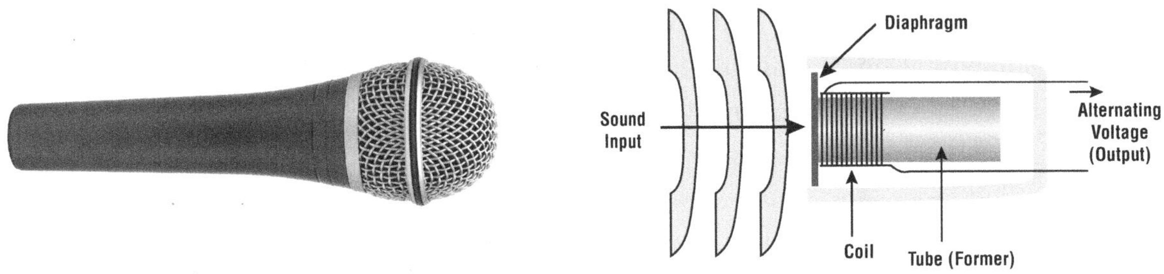

FIG. 1.5. Dynamic Microphone Cross-Section

Speakers

Speakers are electromechanical transducers that reverse the process and turn electrical signals back into acoustic sound. Speaker systems can use more than one driver element in order to cover as much of the audible frequency spectrum as possible. The make and manufacture of the various components in a speaker enclosure can affect the sound and cause discrepancies in the way producers hear their compositions.

The drivers are named sub-woofer, woofer, mid-range speaker, tweeter, and super tweeter, covering the respective frequencies from the low 20 Hz to the high 20,000 Hz. The most common of these elements are the woofer, mid-range speaker, and tweeter which simplifies the full band to just three ranges: bass, mid-range, and hi (or treble), which are commonly seen in consumer equipment.

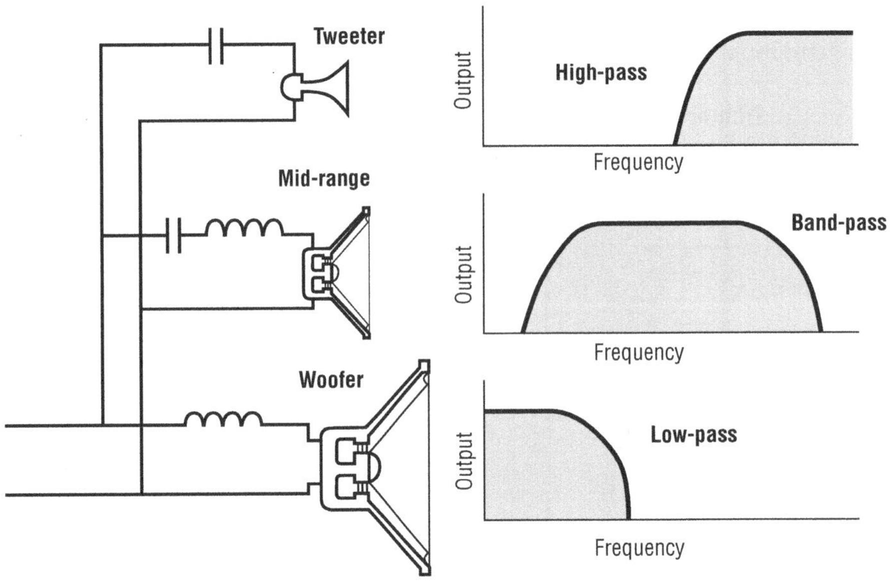

FIG. 1.6. Multi-Driver Speaker

Headphones

Headphones are small loudspeakers, such as earphones or earbuds. In recording studios, the slang term "cans" are also used. Headphones are "close to the ear" speakers that connect to electronic audio sources such as audio amplifiers, radios, CD players, MP3 players, and more.

FIG. 1.7. Studio Headphones vs. Earbuds

INSTRUMENT IDENTIFICATION AND MICROPHONE CHOICE

Being able to accurately *identify* (i.e., capture and render) a wide variety of instrument sounds makes it easier to include interesting sounds in a hip-hop production. Most hip-hop producers will eventually study the sound of individual drums (kick, snare, hi-hat, rack toms, floor tom, crash cymbal, ride cymbal), ambient drums (one or two microphones recording an entire drum kit), basses, keyboards and synthesizers, guitars, horns, strings, and percussion.

In order to capture the unique identity of each instrument sound, producers use a variety of different microphones when recording live instruments for hip-hop, and I'll give you a short list of some of what I have found to be more or less standard practice in commercial recording studios.

Vocals

I use a single condenser microphone for singers and rappers: the Sony C800G or the AKG C12, usually in a cardioid pattern. If there are plosive b's or p's (a buildup of the proximity effect due to the pressure gradient nature of the cardioid polar pattern), I will record a second pass using an omni pattern (which exhibits no buildup of the proximity effect due to the pressure sensitive nature of the omni polar pattern), and edit the plosives out with pieces from the new vocal recording. The range of human voices can be from a low of 82 Hz for the bottom range of bass singers to 1,046 Hz for the top range of soprano singers. (See figure 13.1 for more about vocal ranges.) Both of these microphone polar patterns capture vocals well across male and female frequency ranges.

Drum Kit

Audio 1.1
Kick Drum

The following are suggested areas to begin looking at frequency response in drums. Actual frequencies vary by drum size and manufacturing material.

- Kick: Electro-Voice RE20. The kick has an initial *transient* (a fast onset, short duration peak) that is in the neighborhood of 5,000 Hz and a resonant cavity tone that is in the neighborhood of 50 Hz.

Audio 1.2
Snare Drum

- Snare: Shure SM57. The snare has a transient in the neighborhood of 3,000 Hz and a resonant cavity in the neighborhood of 200 Hz.

Audio 1.3a
Hi-Hat Closed

Audio 1.3b
Hi-Hat Closed and Open

- Hi-hat: AKG 451. Hi-hat energy is in the neighborhood of about 8,000 Hz.

Audio 1.4
Hi, Mid, and Low Toms

- Toms: Sennheiser MD 421. Toms (i.e., tom-toms) augment the kick drum and the snare drum, with larger toms having transients in the neighborhood of 3,000 to 5,000 Hz and resonant cavities from 50 to 200 Hz, to smaller toms with progressively higher frequencies.

Audio 1.5
Ride Cymbal, Bright Crash, and Dark Crash

- Overheads: two AKG 451s using a stereo microphone configuration. Crash, splash, ride, and sizzle cymbals contain high-frequency energy in the area of 6,000 to 12,000 Hz.

Percussion

Audio 1.6
Congas, Cowbell, Shaker, Hand Claps, and Finger Snaps

There are wide ranges of instruments that live in the percussion family. Because of the fast-moving transients of percussion, dynamic microphones such as the Shure SM58 and SM57 microphones can do a great job. Basically, anything that can be struck can be considered a percussion instrument. From actual drums to boxes to walls, cups, and bowls, percussion instruments are at the forefront of keeping time and adding rhythm to songs. The frequency responses vary depending on the size and density of the thing being struck, and the size and density of the thing doing the striking. In the case of hip-hop, you can think of tambourines, hand claps, congas, bongos, cow bells, triangles, and wind chimes as the leading candidates in this category, with frequency ranges from about 200 Hz to about 12,000 Hz.

Piano

Audio 1.7
Piano

Piano is typically mic'd using either a single microphone for a mono image or a pair of microphones for a stereo image pointing at the center of the keyboards strings.

I use two AKG C414s, using a coincident stereo X-Y microphone configuration or a near-coincident ORTF configuration. Acoustic pianos usually have eighty-eight keys that span the frequency range from 27.5 to 4,186 Hz.

Bass

Audio 1.8
Bass

The amplifier of a bass guitar is typically mic'd using a single Electro-Voice RE20 dynamic microphone to enhance low frequency response. Bass frequencies range from 41 to 392 Hz (not including harmonics) for a four-string bass and 31 to 523 Hz for a six-string bass.

Guitar

Audio 1.9
Guitar

The amplifier of an electric guitar is typically mic'd using a single dynamic Shure SM57 microphone. Guitar frequencies range from 82 to 1,174 Hz (not including harmonics). Basses and guitars are most often recorded without amplifiers in hip-hop, which yields a recorded signal free of room ambience or amp noise. Basses and guitars are recorded instead using DI (direct injection) boxes that capture the performances directly to recording mediums. Recording with a DI box creates more flexibility over the type of ambience that can be added back to the basses and guitars during the recording and mixing phases of a hip-hop production.

Horns

Horns are typically mic'd using a single condenser microphone for each horn, or varying stereo microphone techniques for a horn section. The classic Neumann U87 is a great microphone for the versatility of a horn section. Horns can range from low baritone sax notes around 69 Hz to high trumpet notes around 932 Hz.

Live horn sections have become rare in contemporary hip-hop. Instead, today, you might hear a single saxophone or trumpet line used thematically throughout the composition. But a properly mic'd horn section can lend your track an old-school sound. Listen to "Super Bad" by James Brown (1970) or "Sexy MF" by Prince (1992) for examples of old school horns.

Strings

Strings are typically mic'd using a single condenser microphone for each stringed instrument, or varying stereo microphone techniques for a string section. The AKG 414 is a wonderful microphone used to capture the complex resonance of string instruments. The low note of a cello is 65 Hz and the higher range of a violin is up to 2,637 Hz. Once again, live string sections, like live horn sections, have become rare in hip-hop, with most producers opting more for synthesizer modeling of string sections. Listen to "It's a Man's Man's Man's World" by James Brown (1966) or Joss Stone's live cover of the same song from 2003 for examples of old school strings.

The preceding microphone choices can be heard on "I'm Going Down" (1994) by Mary J. Blige, which is a cover of Rose Royce's 1976 composition of the same name.

HUMAN FEEL

Another takeaway you should get from studying hip-hop's live band era is human feel. The first programmable digital drum machine had not been commercially released in 1979. All records used drummers, and each drummer imposed natural fluctuations on the tempo of the recording. (There were a few music artists that used preprogrammed rhythm boxes, such as Sly Stone and Parliament Funkadelic, and Roland had been dabbling with a programmable rhythm box since 1972, but *programmable* drum machines would not take off in the music industry for another year yet).

So, what does live feel mean? It means that the tempo of your performance is not as steady as a metronome. Metronomes are devices used by musicians that create a consistent and audible "click" at user defined intervals.

Tempo and Duration

The tempo of a given click is an absolute, empirical measurement, expressed as a measurement in beats per minute. The duration of a musical event or setting is typically measured by audio editing devices in units of milliseconds (ms)—that is, thousandths of a second. Sometimes, in production, we need to convert one measurement to the other.

For music making, we establish tempo as a rate of beats per minute (bpm), not milliseconds, so we need to do a bit of conversion to find the duration of a beat on our metronome (which measures clicks in bpm/beats per minute). This calculation may be needed when setting various production parameters, such as reverb or delay times.

Calculating Durations and Tempos

Here's how that conversion between tempo (measured in beats per minute, bpm) and actual duration (measured in milliseconds, ms) works.

By definition, there are 1,000 ms in a second. There are 60 seconds (s) in a minute. Multiplying 1,000 ms by 60 s reveals the number of milliseconds in a minute: 60,000.

1,000 ms × 60 s = 60,000 ms in a minute

When we subdivide the number of milliseconds in a minute by the number of beats per minute, the duration of one beat in milliseconds is revealed.

60,000 ms in a minute/bpm = the duration of 1 beat in milliseconds

Or simply

60,000/bpm = 1 beat (ms)

So, one beat at 60 bpm lasts for 1,000 milliseconds.

60,000 ms/60 bpm = 1,000 ms per beat

Or, one beat at 90 bpm lasts for 666.7 ms.

60,000 ms/90 bpm = 666.7ms per beat

Or, one beat at 120 bpm lasts for 500 ms per beat.

60,000 ms/120 bpm = 500 ms per beat

Again, this formula can be used to set delay times and reverb lengths in your time-based effects. Here, for example, is a look at a 1,000 ms reverb setting in a DAW.

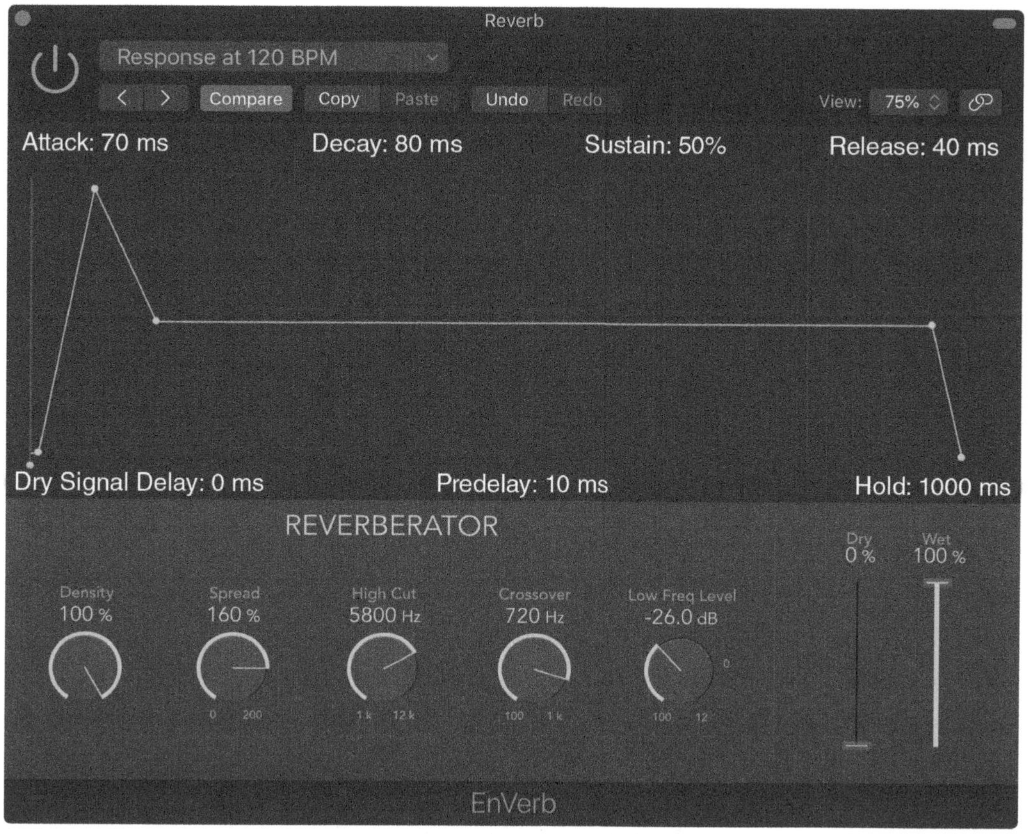

FIG. 1.8. Reverb Settings at 120 bpm Holding for Two Beats (1,000 ms)

If you know the duration of a beat, you can cross multiply this formula to find the tempo of your composition.

60,000 ms in 1 minute/the duration of 1 beat in milliseconds = bpm

For instance, if each beat has a duration of 1,000 milliseconds, the tempo is 60 bpm.

60,000/1,000 equals 60 bpm

If each beat has a duration of 500 milliseconds, the tempo is 120 bpm.

60,000/500 = 120 bpm

When you are resolving the tempo using bars instead of beats, you multiply the numerator by 4 (beats).

60,000 ms × 4 beats/the duration one bar in milliseconds = bpm

For instance, if each bar has a duration of 4,000 milliseconds, the tempo is 60 bpm.

60,000 ms × 4/4,000 ms = 60 bpm

If each bar has a duration of 2,222, the tempo is 108 bpm.

60,000 ms × 4/2,222 ms = 108 bpm

Drummers usually play the drum kit while listening to a metronome but drummers are not machines so their performances will contain minor fluctuations. When the drummer's time fluctuates, the bpm changes from bar to bar and even beat to beat. An analysis of the first sixteen bars of "Rapper's Delight" reveals differing tempos for each bar (a section that contains four beats):

Bar 1	**Bar 2**	**Bar 3**	**Bar 4**
108.0	109.0	109.9	106.5
Bar 5	**Bar 6**	**Bar 7**	**Bar 8**
108.4	108.9	108.1	110.2
Bar 9	**Bar 10**	**Bar 11**	**Bar 12**
109.8	112.2	110.5	111.8
Bar 13	**Bar 14**	**Bar 15**	**Bar 16**
109.9	112.6	111.2	112.3

FIG. 1.9. Tempo Fluctuations in "Rapper's Delight"

If the drummer played "Rapper's Delight" as steadily as a metronome, the tempos would look like figure 1.10, and it would have lost its live-performance feel:

Bar 1	**Bar 2**	**Bar 3**	**Bar 4**
108.0	108.0	108.0	108.0
Bar 5	**Bar 6**	**Bar 7**	**Bar 8**
108.0	108.0	108.0	108.0
Bar 9	**Bar 10**	**Bar 11**	**Bar 12**
108.0	108.0	108.0	108.0
Bar 13	**Bar 14**	**Bar 15**	**Bar 16**
108.0	108.0	108.0	108.0

FIG. 1.10. Metronomic Performance

"The Breaks" tempos similarly vary, and it looks like this:

Bar 1	**Bar 2**	**Bar 3**	**Bar 4**
111.7	113.9	113.7	112.0
Bar 5	**Bar 6**	**Bar 7**	**Bar 8**
113.2	114.4	112.5	114.8
Bar 9	**Bar 10**	**Bar 11**	**Bar 12**
112.2	115.1	112.6	114.7
Bar 13	**Bar 14**	**Bar 15**	**Bar 16**
112.9	114.2	112.9	112.8

FIG. 1.11. Tempo Fluctuations in "The Breaks"

In the preceding figures:

- **Bar:** One measure (grouping) of four clicks/beats, when you are counting in 4/4 time (typical of hip-hop).
- **Tempo:** the number of beats in sixty seconds of time (i.e., beats per minute, bpm).

Our charts resolve to a tenth of a beat per minute, so a tempo of 111.7 bpm is faster than 111 bpm but slower than 112 bpm. Early hip-hop tempos ranged between 100 and 120 bpm. This allowed the compositions to maintain danceability as well as a moderate enough speed for articulating syllables.

When compared to a "general" tempo chart of other genres, early hip-hop tempos are relatively dance-oriented because of their up-tempo nature:

GENERIC STYLE	BPM AVERAGE	BPM RANGE
Dance	120	105–135
Mid Tempo	90	75–105
Ballad	60	45–75

FIG. 1.12. A General Tempo Chart

ACTIVITIES CHAPTER 1

Listening

Using your favorite playback app, listen to "Good Times" by Chic, "Rapper's Delight" by the Sugarhill Gang, and "The Breaks" by Kurtis Blow. Make note of the stereo imaging, instrument choices, and tempos. What are the similarities and differences between these compositions? When you feel that you have sufficiently analyzed these compositions, move on to the production exercises for this chapter.

Production

The online media (see the first page of this book for how to access it) includes an instrumental composition that reflects concepts discussed in this chapter. There is also a folder containing the individual audio files of each instrument within the composition. You can import these audio files to your DAW for mixing practice and/or recording your own rap performances in the style of the live band era.

Download

DAW Track 1.10 PC's Delight

1. **Listen to the beat.** Import the stereo mix of "PC's Delight" to your DAW. Listen for the human feel of the beat, and list the instruments that you hear.
2. **Rap to the beat.** Import the stereo mix of "PC's Delight" to your DAW. Add the rap lyrics of "Rapper's Delight," recorded on a separate track.
3. **Rap to the separated files of the beat.** Import the individual files to have control over each sound. Rap the lyrics of "Rapper's Delight" recorded on a separate track. Mix to taste.
4. **Create your own beat.** Use live instruments and/or the virtual instruments in your DAW to create your own beat and original rap that sounds like the live band era in hip hop.

CHAPTER 2

Drum Machines and Synthesizers: 1981 to 1983

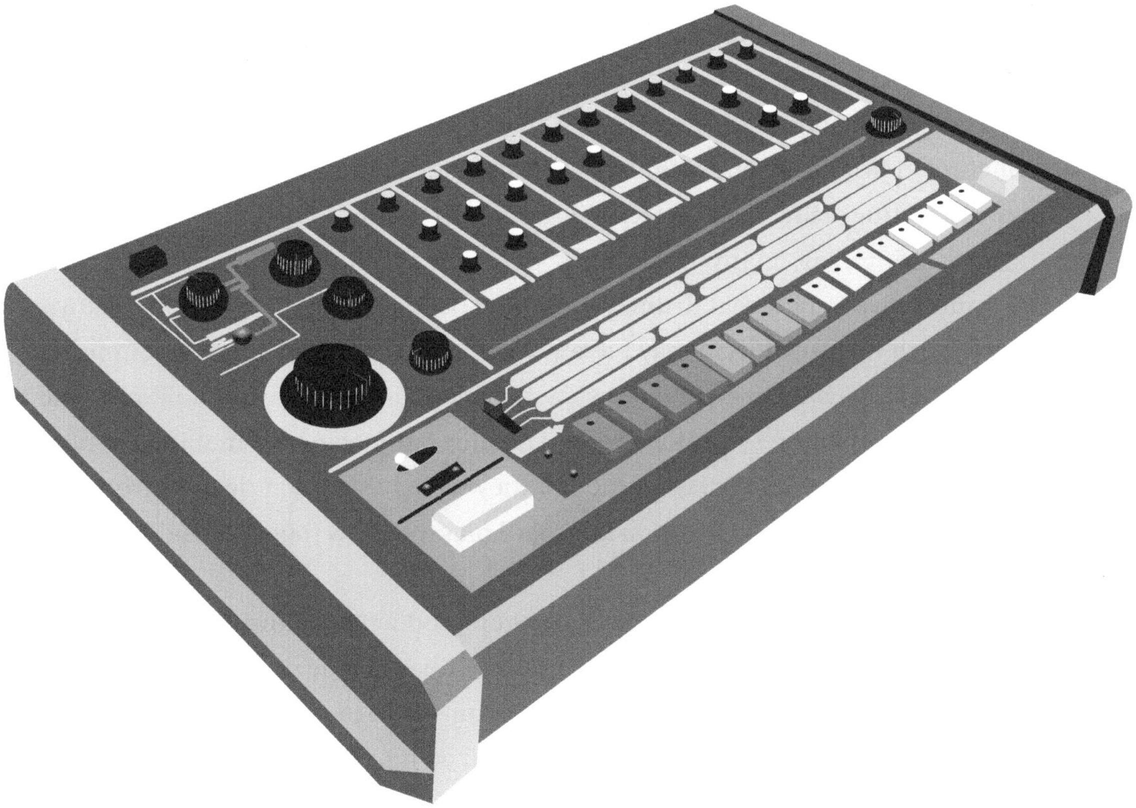

LISTENING:

- "Trans-Europe Express" by Kraftwerk (1977)
- "Planet Rock" by Afrika Bambaataa and the Soulsonic Force (1982)
- "The Message" by Grandmaster Flash and the Furious Five (1982)
- "It's Like That" by Run DMC (1983)

DRUM MACHINES

In 1980, two drum machines were released that would change the sound of hip-hop—and eventually, modern music in general.

The first was the Linn LM-1 Drum Computer. It was the first drum machine using digital samples that allowed you to program your own rhythms.

The other was the Roland TR-808 Rhythm Composer. It used simple synthesizer tones (sine waves and triangle waves) mixed with white noise passing through a sound shaping envelope to create interesting percussive sounds. Its rhythms were also programmable.

Early approaches by musicians to use these programmable drum machines usually resulted in a conventional approach, as a sort of electronic mimicking of an actual drummer. Hip-hop producers saw a different opportunity for the application of the drum machine's programmable rhythms. For example, listen to the cyclical approach used on "It's Like That," released in late 1983 by Run DMC. It features the drum machine and synthesizer as the main focal points of the composition, with a percussive performance devoid of a hi-hat and punctuated with a cyclical two-bar tom-tom fill—not necessarily something that would satiate the musical chops of a well-studied drummer, but definitely characteristic of the way hip-hop producers were innovating, using the new technologies of that period.

Needless to say, many drummers were not too fond of drum machines. Drummers love to play real drums, and many perceived drum machines as toys. Even though manufacturers may have wanted to sell a ton of drum machines to all musicians, early drum machines were most popular with keyboard players who were already exploring sound synthesis. The programmable beat-making strength of the LM-1 and the TR-808, even though they were based on a rigid metronomic time base, gave the hip-hop session keyboard players a new tool to introduce to the rappers they were working with.

From 1980 to 1983, more and more hip-hop productions moved away from live band recordings in favor of recording drum machines to tape as the basic rhythmic body of their compositions. All the other instrument parts, which quickly became just keyboard and synthesizer parts, were added on top of the programmed beat.

Audio 2.1 Linn Drum Sounds

FIG. 2.1. Linn LM-1 Drum Computer

Linn Electronics. Successor: Forat Electronics - Bruce Forat, president, Linn LM-1 Drum Computer large.jpg, CC BY-SA 3.0, https://commons.wikimedia.org/wiki/File:Linn_LM-1_Drum_Computer_large.jpg

Audio 2.2 TR-808 Sounds

FIG. 2.2. TR-808 Rhythm Composer

Brandon Daniel. Derivative work: Clusternote (talk), Roland_TR-808_&_909.jpg, CC-BY-SA 2.0, https://commons.wikimedia.org/wiki/File:Roland_TR-808_(large).jpg

Another entry in early hip-hop drum machine folklore is the Oberheim DMX (released in 1981), which was, at that time, the most affordable of the digital drum machines at $2,895. Even though the Linn LM-1 was the first programmable digital drum machine, the Oberheim DMX is heard on a huge amount of hip-hop from this period because of its affordability.

FIG. 2.3. Oberheim DMX
https://www.matrixsynth.com/2013/11/oberheim-dmx-vintage-drum-machine-with.htmlProgramming Drum Machines

Audio 2.3 Oberheim DMX Sounds

There are two ways to program a drum machine (or any sequencer for that matter).

1. In *real time*, you strike different contact points on the unit in time to an audible metronome generated by the machine's internal *sequencer* (the device that records).
2. In *step time*, you select the exact beat or sub-beat on which you want the performance to occur, based on a grid that resembles the mathematical partitioning of rhythms in music notation. This grid-type system is the building block of a simple drum machine, and this simple *step sequencing* process paved the way for later advances such as MIDI and music sequencing.

A simple step sequencer will control tempo, start, stop, and volume (of individual sounds), and it will have some way to store user patterns. Most drum machines are step sequencers with built-in sounds. If a machine does not contain a step sequencer, then it is considered a *drum module*, not a drum machine, and would be probably be used in conjunction with a music sequencer.

One of the biggest critiques of drum machines is that they are metronomic; the music will not have a human feel. Though this was initially a perceived flaw, metronomic time—where each beat of a drum machine is in the correct bar/beat position for its chosen tempo, without fluctuation—has become the norm in hip-hop, and popular music.

Step Sequencers

Drum machines, then and now, are the merger of a step sequencer and a playback system that can play either synthesized sounds, samples, or both.

FIG. 2.4. Reason's Redrum. Also a step sequencer.

Step sequencing breaks down a musical bar into beats, and the beats into individual increments that exist along a predetermined time reference.

These increments can usually be viewed on the front panel of a drum machine's step sequencer, and with practice, it will make sense. Step sequencers are used to make short patterns that can then be strung together to form a longer chain of patterns. Hip-hop beat makers use the software program FL Studio in a step-sequencing fashion to create the music beds of many modern hip-hop compositions. Programming can be done by inserting performances into the increments of a prescribed "grid" while the sequencer is not running, or in real time, where you actually play the input device as the metronome (or *click*) is being heard. You can hear this type of grid approach at work on "Crank That" by Soulja Boy from *SouljaBoyTellem* (2007).

SYNTHESIZERS

Once you start making your own beats, you will inevitably want to add interesting sounds to those beats. An overall understanding of synthesizers and synthetic sound modeling will be as useful to you as it was to the keyboard players of the '80s who were hired to play early hip-hop compositions.

Additive synthesis, subtractive synthesis, and FM synthesis are the three types of synthesis that were developing in this early music making period.

Additive Synthesis Waveforms

Additive synthesis combines simple waveforms to create complex waveforms. For example:

- A *sine* wave is a simple fundamental tone with no additional harmonics. It's just a pure tone.
- A *sawtooth* wave is a simple fundamental tone with all the even and odd harmonics at proportionally varying amplitudes to the fundamental, e.g., the second harmonic added at half the amplitude, the third harmonic added at one third the amplitude, and so on.
- A *square* wave is a simple fundamental tone with only the odd harmonics at proportionally varying amplitudes to the fundamental, e.g., the third harmonic added at one third the amplitude, the fifth harmonic added at one fifth the amplitude, and so on.
- A *triangle* wave is a simple fundamental with only the odd harmonics at proportionally varying squared amplitudes, with every other odd harmonic out of phase, e.g., the third harmonic out of phase at one ninth the amplitude, the fifth harmonic in phase at one twenty-fifth amplitude, the seventh harmonic out of phase at one forty-ninth the amplitude, the ninth harmonic in phase at one eighty-first amplitude, the eleventh harmonic out of phase at one one-hundred-twenty-first the amplitude, and so forth.
- A *pulse* wave is a fundamental tone that resembles a rectangular wave but includes a varying duty cycle (period) that can be created by subtracting a sawtooth wave from a phase-shifted version of itself.

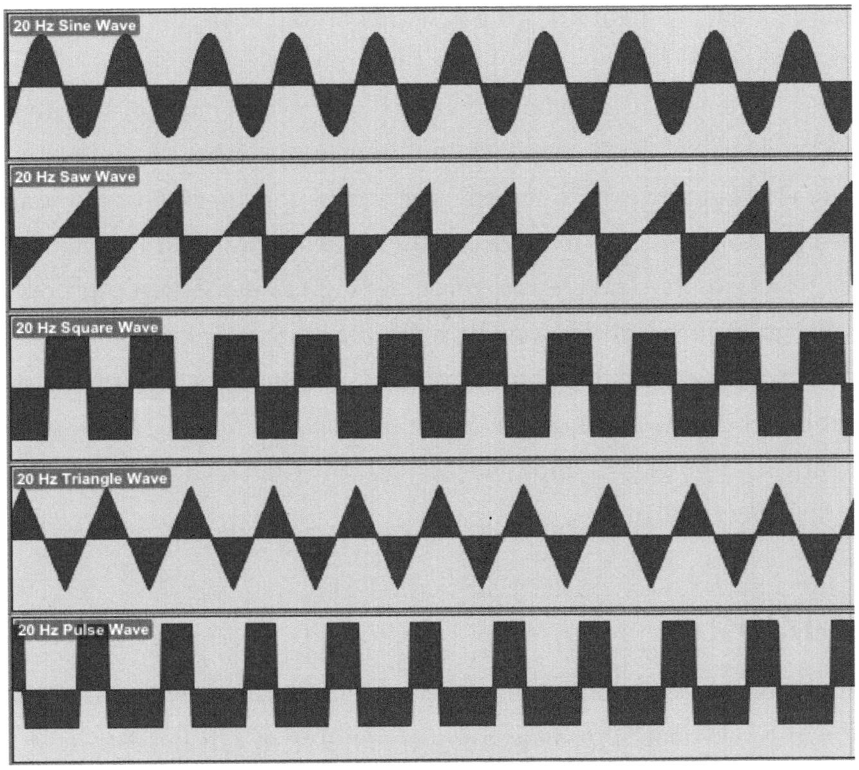

FIG. 2.5. Sine, Saw, Square, Triangle, and Pulse Waveforms

Noise is also used to help add complexity to synthetic sounds. The two most common types of noise are white noise and pink noise:

- *Pink noise* generates equal energy per octave (soft sounding noise).
- *White noise* generates equal energy per frequency (harsh sounding noise).

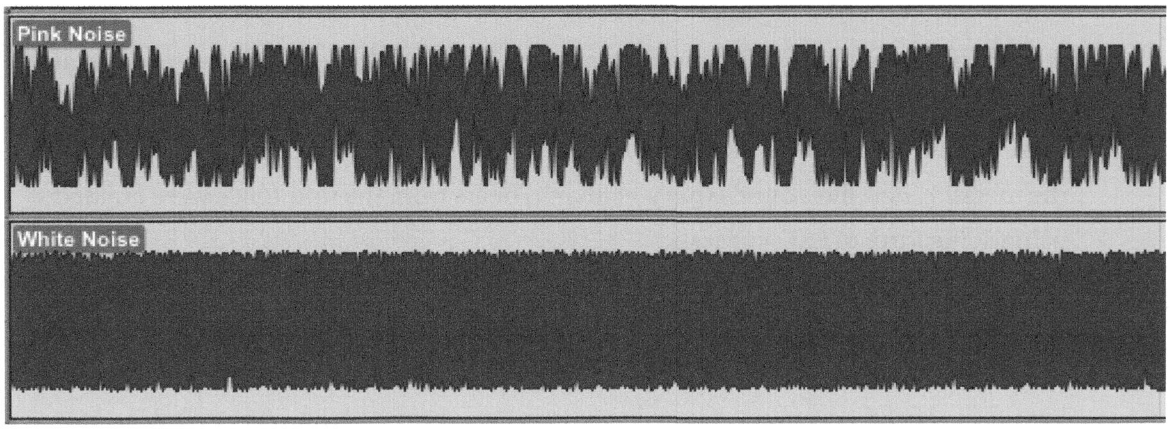

FIG. 2.6. Pink Noise and White Noise

You can open your DAW and find examples of these tones on a synthesizer or a tone generator.

Subtractive Synthesis

By contrast, *subtractive synthesizers* of the early 1980s were smaller and less expensive than additive synthesizers and were the more common synthetic sound-generation tool used in hip-hop. Subtractive synthesis starts with complex waveforms such as saw, square, triangle, and pulse, passing through filters that attenuate the harmonic content. The result is the creation of a simpler waveform from a complex waveform. Simple subtractive synthesizer design includes an *oscillator* (sound source), a *filter* (sound shaper), and an *amplifier* (sound projector). The oscillator, filter, and amplifier can all be modified by the attack, decay, sustain, and release parameters of an *envelope* or by the cyclical variations of an *LFO* (low frequency oscillator).

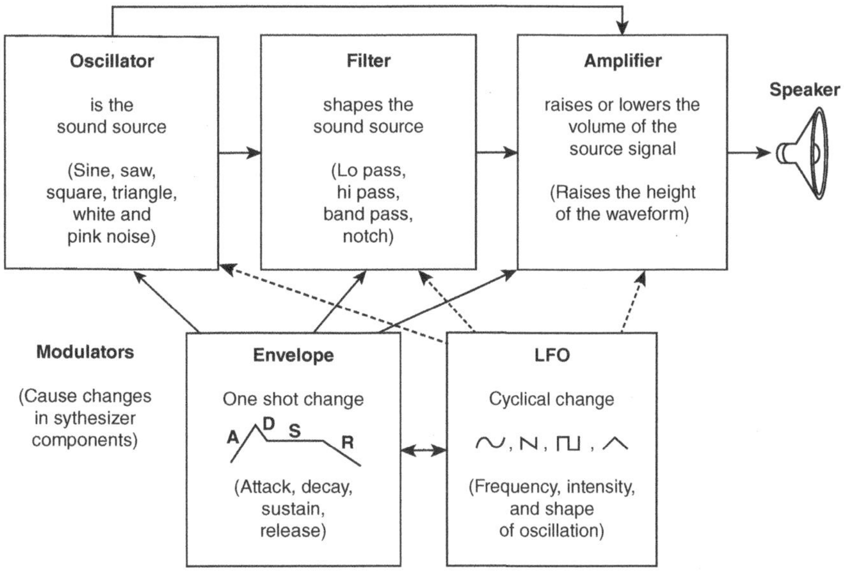

FIG. 2.7. Subtractive Synthesizer Design

FM Synthesis (Frequency Modulation)

In 1983, Yamaha's DX7, using FM synthesis, truly revolutionized the way music sounded. *FM synthesis* (frequency modulation synthesis) creates a complex waveform by modulating a simple waveform (the carrier) with the oscillation of a second simple waveform (the modulator). Varying the oscillations of the modulating waveform by harmonic series per tone, instead of by static oscillations, allowed a musical complexity not afforded by simple additive or subtractive synthesis. Synthetic versions of the Fender Rhodes, the Wurlitzer 200A Electric Piano, as well as many of the metallic, bell-like sounds that you hear in beats from the mid 1980s were created using some form of FM synthesis.

LATER DEVELOPMENTS IN SYNTHESIS

Synthetic design continued beyond the drum machine/synthesizer period, so let's continue the timeline for context surrounding the evolution of synthesizers.

LA Synthesis (Linear Arithmetic)

Another early game changer in synthesis was the Roland D-50, introduced in 1987. Its Linear Arithmetic design offered a collection of internally generated complex waveforms whose attack transient was a digital sample. This enabled some of their synthesized sounds to have an even closer resemblance to acoustic sounds when desired.

Wavetable Synthesis

A type of synthesis that had been around since the 1970s but didn't start showing up in hip-hop until much later was wavetable synthesis. Developed by Palm Products GmbH (PPG), wavetable synthesis is a based around the single cycle of several complex waveforms laid out in a manner that each one can reproduce itself or morph into another of the waveforms over time. There can be hundreds of sounds that use the synthesizer's shaping parameters to morph into complex variations. Instruments such as Logic's ES2 use a combination of subtractive, FM, and wavetable synthesis to shape sounds that show up in hip-hop songs from the '80s to the present.

By the turn of the twenty-first century, digital synthesizers had replaced much of the early analog technology, but many hip-hop producers still love working with the "analog sounds" of yesteryear. Today's manufacturers have been satiating these desires with new products that are using vintage analog circuitry in their designs. A recording like "Blow" (2013) by Beyoncé, produced by hip-hop producer Pharrell Williams, is a good example of a recent deep dive into analog circuitry, as is "24K Magic" (2016) by Bruno Mars. Each of these recordings uses concepts honed in the mid 1980s that have been brought back in hip-hop influenced pop compositions.

ACTIVITIES CHAPTER 2

Listening

Using your favorite playback app, listen to "Trans-Europe Express" by Kraftwerk (1977), "Planet Rock" by Afrika Bambaataa and the Soulsonic Force (1982), "The Message" by Grandmaster Flash and the Furious Five (1982), and "It's Like That" by Run DMC (1983). Make note of the stereo imaging, instrument choices, and tempos. What are the similarities and differences between these compositions? What are the similarities and differences between these compositions and the compositions from the previous chapter? Can you identify the type of drum machine (Linn or 808 or DMX)? Can you identify the synthesizer sounds? Can you recreate the synthesizer sounds with your production setup? When you feel that you have sufficiently analyzed these compositions, move on to the production exercises for this chapter.

Production

Download

DAW Track 2.4 PC's Like That

Access the practice files for these activities via the link and code on the first page of this book.

1. **Listen to the beat.** Import the stereo mix of "PC's Like That" to your DAW. Listen for the metronomic feel of the beat, and list the instruments you hear.
2. **Rap to the beat.** Import the stereo mix of "PC's Like That" to your DAW. Add the rap the lyrics of "It's Like That" recorded on a separate track.
3. **Rap to the separated files of the beat.** Import the individual files to have control over each sound. Rap the lyrics of "It's Like That" on a separate track. Mix to taste.
4. **Create your own beat.** Use the virtual instruments in your DAW to create your own beat and rap that sounds like the drum machine and synthesizers era in hip-hop.

CHAPTER 3

MIDI and Sequencing: 1983 to 1987

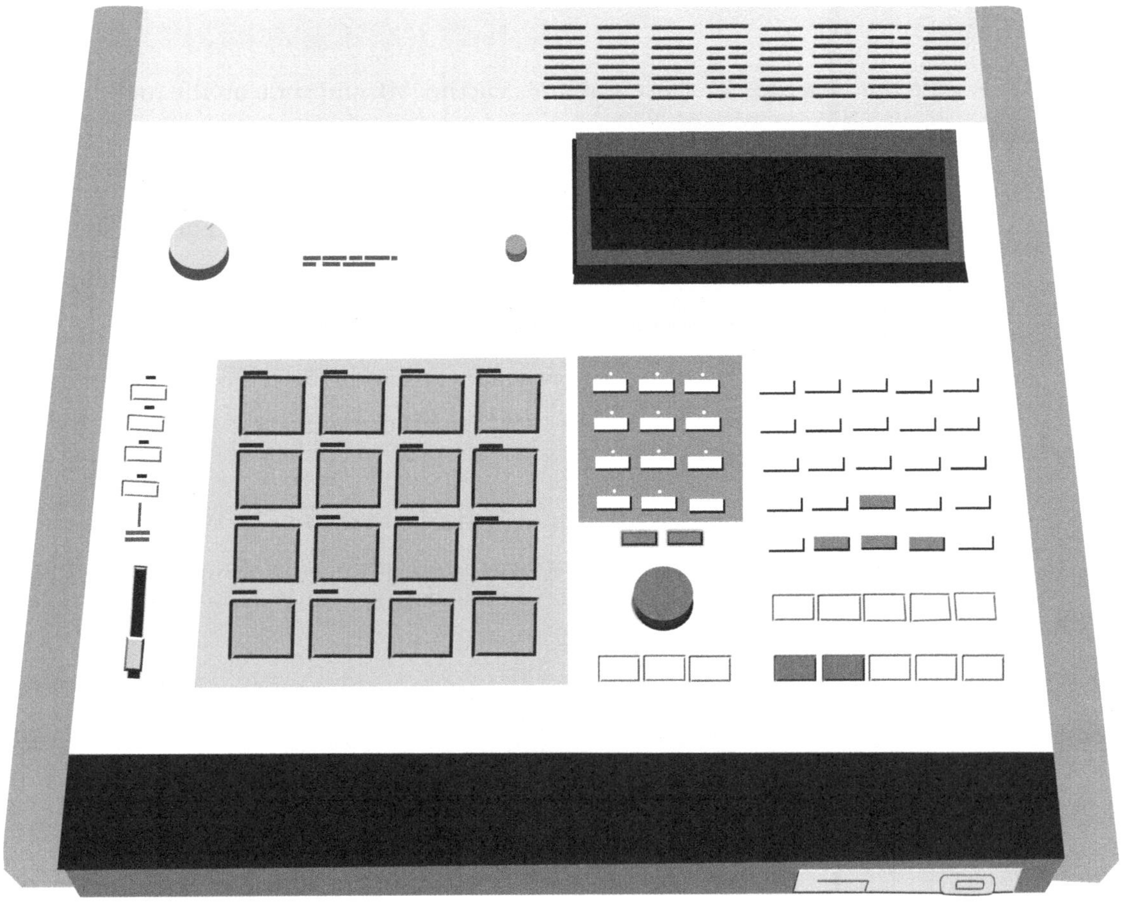

LISTENING: MIDI/SEQUENCING-BASED HIP-HOP

- "The Freaks Come Out at Night" by Whodini (1984)
- "Push It" by Salt-N-Pepa (1987)

WHAT IS MIDI?

MIDI is the acronym for Musical Instrument Digital Interface. Introduced in 1981, and finally published in 1983 by Dave Smith (Sequential Circuits) and Ikutaro Kakehashi (Roland Corp.), MIDI is a technical standard that describes a communications protocol allowing devices that adhere to that standard to easily communicate with each other. It does not transmit audio, but rather digital data in the form of event messages: note on, note off, pitch, velocity, duration, volume, vibrato, panning, and clock signals for tempo and/or timeline. The audio itself is stored on, and then drawn from, the device (such as a sound module) that receives the MIDI direction.

The MIDI protocol enables computers, synthesizers, controllers, sound modules, sound cards, samplers, and drum machines—from various manufacturers—to communicate with each other. It is the revolution that changed music from a group endeavor to a one-person operation and is the life source of modern hip-hop production.

MIDI-based musical performances are digitally described as a series of actions. Those actions then live under one of four messaging types: channel voice, channel mode, system common, or system real time. (Reference the MIDI spec at www.midi.org.)

Early MIDI communication was done through a five-pin DIN (Deutsches Institut für Normung) cable, transmitted at 31.25 kbit/sec, and contained sixteen MIDI channels, each of which was capable of transmitting all of the data events and messaging types. Current MIDI products can instead communicate through USB, Firewire, and wireless Bluetooth transmissions. The MIDI protocol is written into the computer code of most music software, and it can communicate internally or externally when paired with the correct transmission devices.

Once your workflow is in place, you will create performance data that will move from your controller to your sequencer and then be distributed to your sound modules. The data created from MIDI transmission can be saved in a *Standard MIDI File* (SMF), which uses a .mid extension. The data in that file can then be stored or transferred to other MIDI devices.

MODERN MIDI SETUP

The main components of beat making using a modern MIDI setup are the *controller*, the *sound module*, and the *sequencer*. These are the fundamentals—similar to knowing that a rhythm section typically includes a bass, drum set, and piano or guitar.

Controllers

A *controller* is the device that initiates the MIDI communication and can be struck, plucked, strummed, or blown into, depending on the type of controller that you are using. Keyboard controllers and drum controllers are the most successful because they both use a striking motion that is easily tracked in the MIDI data stream. There are also wind controllers and guitar controllers that have a more complicated task of translation than keyboard or drum controllers do, because vibrations in wind and string instruments do not adhere to simple binary on/off convention. Envelopes, gates, and modulation are more at play on these types of MIDI controllers. There are also *MIDI pickups*, which are small devices that attach usually to some type of percussive instrument.

FIG. 3.1. MIDI Controllers. A keyboard controller, a drum pad controller, a wind controller, and a guitar controller.

Sound Modules

Sound modules are the audio voices of the MIDI production model. Also referred to as "tone generators," dedicated sound modules have no playable controller interface, but are instead freestanding devices whose sole job is to play back sounds. Their digital counterparts in today's DAW culture are called "virtual instruments."

A sound module can be a synthesizer, a sampler, or a rompler. A *rompler* (the contraction of ROM [Read Only Memory] and sampler) plays back samples but cannot actually record new sounds. Technically, the LM-1 and DMX drum machines were romplers).

Although contemporary software sound libraries give the modern beat maker a vast number of enough interesting sounds and editing parameters to work with, many hip-hop producers still prefer having a few vintage instruments lying around.

Sequencers

The *sequencer* is the brain of the MIDI production model. The sequencer records the intricate MIDI commands sent from the controller and distributes those commands among various sound modules in the hardware and software realms. Without a sequencer, you could still use your controller to communicate with your sound module, but you couldn't store the MIDI data that was being generated.

Bars and beats are the building blocks of your hip-hop composition, or MIDI "sequence." The *timing clock* (System Real Time parameter) breaks a quarter note up into 24 pulses, or 24 PPQN (pulses per quarter note). This is the smallest increment of relative time between quarter notes in the MIDI protocol. With 24 pulses per quarter note, you can create subdivisions at the eighth note, eighth-note triplet, sixteenth note, sixteenth-note triplet, thirty-second note, and thirty-second-note triplet.

One of the most popular sequencers in hip-hop is the MPC. (Originally called the MIDI Production Center, the acronym now stands for Music Production Center.) The earliest MPC multiplied the resolution of MIDI beat clock by 4, resulting in a timing clock of 96 PPQN. The added increments allowed for a unique feature called swing on the MPC units, where the second and fourth sixteenth notes could be shifted to a different relative position than the first and third sixteenth notes in a musical pattern.

The MPC also contains a drum pad controller and a sampler/sound module. This device, first released by Akai in 1988, has been the main tool for many hip-hop producers and is integral to a huge number of successful recordings in hip-hop. The time divisions of music sequencing will be covered more comprehensively in chapter 6.

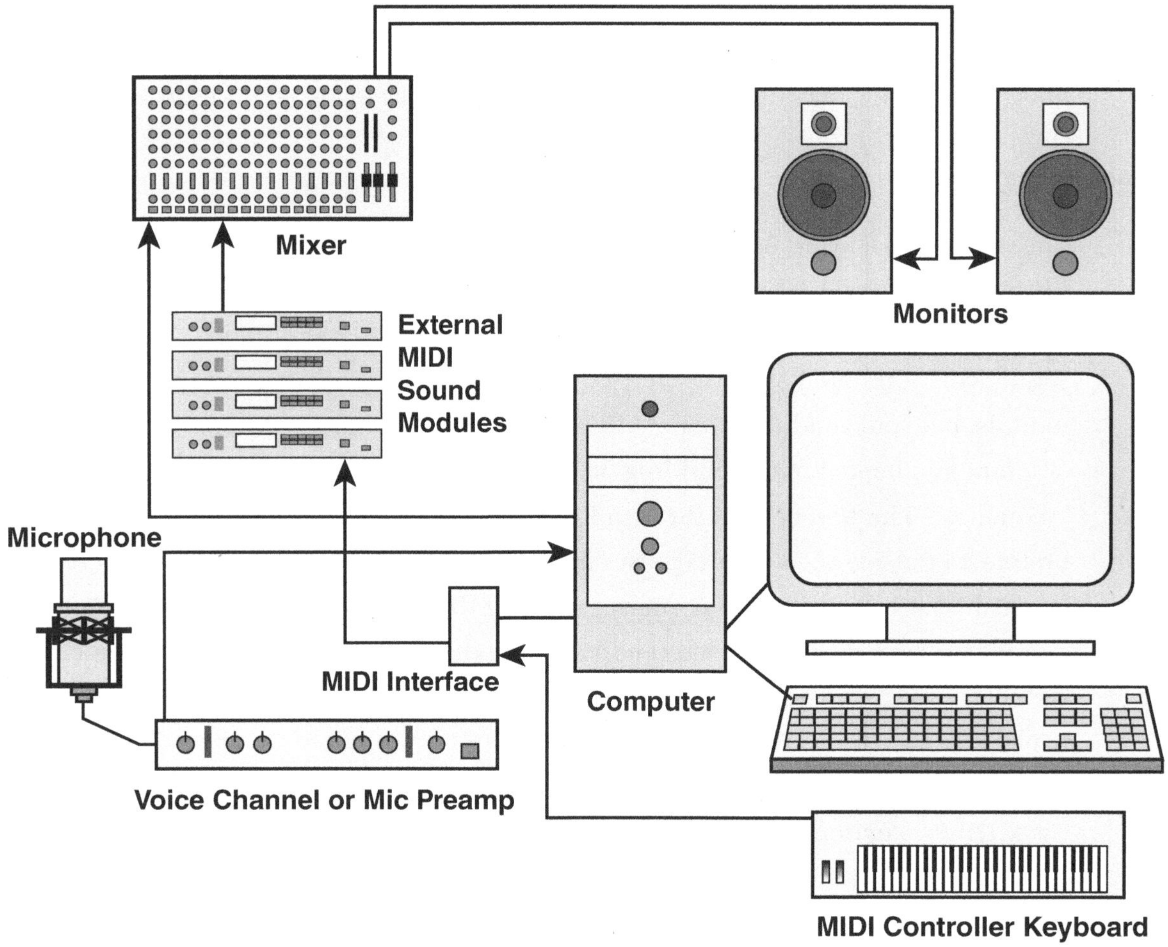

FIG. 3.2. Software MIDI Production Setup from the MMA (MIDI Manufacturer's Association)

ACTIVITIES CHAPTER 3

Listening

Using your favorite playback app, listen to "Freaks Come Out at Night" by Whodini and "Push It" by Salt-N-Pepa. Make note of the stereo imaging, instrument choices, and tempos. What are the similarities and differences between these compositions? What are the similarities and differences between these compositions and the compositions from the previous chapter? Can you identify or recreate the quantized sixteenth-note patterns of the performances with your production setup? When you feel that you have sufficiently analyzed these compositions, move on to the production exercises for this chapter.

Production

Download

DAW Track 3.1
PC Comes Out At Night

Access the practice files for these activities via the link and code on the first page of this book.

1. **Listen to the beat.** Import the stereo mix of "PC Comes Out at Night" to your DAW. Listen for the quantized rhythms of the MIDI performances, and list the instruments you hear.
2. **Rap to the beat.** Import the stereo mix of "PC Comes Out At Night" to your DAW. Rap the lyrics of "Freaks Come Out at Night" recorded on a separate track.
3. **Rap to the separated files of the beat.** Import the individual files to have control over each sound. Rap the lyrics of "Freaks Come Out at Night" on a separate track. Mix to taste.
4. **Create your own beat.** Use the virtual instruments in your DAW to create your own beat and rap that sounds like the MIDI and sequencing era in hip-hop.

CHAPTER 4

Sampling: 1987 to Present

LISTENING: SAMPLING-BASED HIP-HOP

- "It's My Thing" by Marva Whitney (1969) and
- "Get Off Your Ass and Jam" by Funkadelic (1975), which became
- **"Bring the Noise" by Public Enemy (1988)**
- "Funky Drummer" by James Brown and the J.B.'s (1970) and
- "It's My Thing" (again) by Marva Whitney (1969), which became
- **"F*** tha Police" by N.W.A (1989)**
- "Alone Again (Naturally)" by Gilbert O'Sullivan (1971), which became
- **"Alone Again" (1991) by Biz Markie**

"These talking machines are going to ruin the artistic development of music in this country." Do you know who made that famous statement? It was John Philip Sousa in 1906 before a congressional committee on copyright reform, deriding Edison's phonograph. Sampling, too, has had its criticisms, and lawsuits.

A *sample* is an excerpt from a recording, which hip-hop producers often incorporate into new compositions, often via a device called a "sampler." A sample can be as short as a single note or extended to encompass an entire section of a record.

When affordable samplers became available, hip-hop producers who were still using turntables in their live performances found a new tool to explore. Samplers gave them the ability to lift musical samples from soul and funk artists such as James Brown, Marva Whitney, Rufus Thomas and many others. The albums *It Takes a Nation of Millions to Hold Us Back* (1988) and *Fear of a Black Planet* (1990), by Public Enemy, ushered in a sound that was an audio explosion. The sound was loved, hated, discussed, dismissed, empowering, and controversial. Sampling, and the intricate way the samples were organized by the production team, screamed innovation and a new kind of *technical soul power* into the face of critics and copyright infringement in 1988.

Just as Sylvia Robinson had to figure how to navigate copyright issues, the new generation of producers who began exploiting the use of sampling in their compositions would have to face the same scrutiny. Was the final sampled product a new entity with a brand-new claim to copyright? Or, did the existing copyright of the song being sampled hold up as an original composition that needed to be defended by the Copyright Act of 1976? The debate on sampling rages to this day, and a novel concept called the *sample clearance division* started springing up at record companies to address this new innovation in hip-hop. The art form was going boldly toward what early hip-hop music makers had shied away from: the published recording itself.

Iconic cases like *Grand Upright Music, Ltd. v. Warner Bros. Records, Inc.*, demanded that hip-hop producers credit and compensate the original creators of their sampled works of published material. In one of the most famous cases in hip-hop lore, Biz Markie's "Alone Again" (1991) was cited for copyright infringement of Gilbert O'Sullivan's "Alone Again (Naturally)" (1972). Not only did Mr. O'Sullivan not want his work used by Biz Markie; he did not want his work associated with hip-hop—even if he was credited. That was ruled to be his legal right.

Many artists who embarked on a sampling frenzy during this era eventually had to pay the piper and fork over their royalties and profits to the original songwriters.

Let's look at the idea of sampling differently, because again, creating new music out of pre-existing music actually is not a new concept. Borrowing music has been a practice used in the creation of music since music began. Here are four different ways to recontextualize the word "sampling":

1. Sampling as *INSPIRATION*. You listen, and then seek to create in response to what you have heard, without much regard to the specific instrumentation or melodic invention of the original reference. Is it possible that David Bowie's "Space Oddity" (1969) may have inspired Elton John's "Rocket Man" (1972)? This does not present any glaring legal issues.
2. Sampling as *EMULATION*, or suggestive of another artist within a genre. You listen to and then consciously use the instrumentation and melodic devices of a specific artist or composition within a certain genre. For instance, Lady Gaga's "Born This Way" (2011) feels like it has borrowed strains from many of Madonna's older hits, including "Express Yourself" (1989), "Vogue" (1990), and "Ray of Light" (1998). On the surface, this is not legally problematic and is probably how a huge percentage of music is created. But in 2015, "Blurred Lines" (2013) by Robin Thicke was legally found to have infringed on the copyright of "Got to Give It Up" (1977) by Marvin Gaye. This was appealed in 2016, and an amicus curae brief was presented from more than 200 musicians and producers in support of the appeal. In March 2018, the United States Court of Appeals for the Ninth Circuit upheld the original ruling of the United States District Court for the Central District of California that the copyright had been violated.
3. Sampling as *INTERPOLATION*. You take the very elements from another artist or composition and rework them into a new composition using live elements, MIDI, DJ sampling, or electronic sampling. You then introduce new sonic, melodic, and lyrical inventions to complete the process of interpolation. Listen to "La Bamba" (1958) by Richie Valens and compare it to "Twist and Shout" (1963) by the Beatles. Do you hear any similarities in the intro and melodic lines? A large body of hip-hop work falls squarely into this category, from the Sugarhill Gang's "Rapper's Delight," which we saw uses the musical structure of Chic's "Good Times," to Snoop Dogg's "Who Am I (What's My Name)" (1993), a reworking of Parliament's "Give Up The Funk (Tear The Roof Off The Sucker)" (1976), Funkadelic's "Knee Deep" (1979) and George Clinton's "Atomic Dog" (1982). Interpolation is not problematic if the original copyright holder has granted you permission to use their work. If you have not been granted that permission, then you are infringing on the legal copyright of another creative artist. There are many famous copyright infringement cases. One of the most famous was the aforementioned *Grand Upright Music, Ltd. v. Warner Bros. Records, Inc.*
4. Sampling as *DUPLICATION*. This is also called a "cover" of a composition or "covering" a composition. You remake, or cover, another artist's song or rendition of a song. An example of this would be the huge hip-hop smash "Walk This Way" (1986) by Run DMC, which is a hip-hop duplication of Aerosmith's "Walk This Way" (1975). If you have been granted permission by the original copyright holder, duplication is not problematic. If that permission has not been granted, you are in violation of another creative artist's copyright. Social media services police their platforms for the broadcasting of compositions by non copyright holders.

These interpretations of the word "sampling" may help you look at the creative connections found by hip-hop producers in a different way. *Creative sampling* is more than just using technological tools. It begins in (1) the mind of the producer as imagination derived from inspired sources; (2) the desire to emulate a piece of art that has already touched the soul of his or her creative spirit; (3) the outright interpolation of a great song, dressed with new, contemporary elements; or (4) the spiritual homage to an admired artist and that artist's composition.

SAMPLERS AND MICRO-SAMPLERS

Before the Bomb Squad work of 1987, sampling technology was already being used as a tool in recording studios. Music producers and engineers would use previously recorded material in their creative works to expand their creative textures. The Beatles, for example, used other records' instrument sounds, sound effects, and vocal performances on the album *Yellow Submarine* (1966).

When I interviewed Hank Shocklee from the Bomb Squad, the producer of Public Enemy, he told me that he also used tape machines in his early sampling work. But the first studio devices dedicated to sampling in hip-hop (samplers) were simple signal-processing devices used by engineers, using audio triggers to replace elements such as snare and kick drums. One of those devices was the DMX 15-80 S released in 1978 by Advanced Music Systems (AMS). It could be used to play a recorded sample that was triggered by a different sound coming from a tape machine.

This small type of sample is called a *micro-sample*. Because micro-samples don't take up a lot of digital space, Roger Linn used the same short sampling idea effectively within his LinnDrum in 1980. The LinnDrum, however, did not offer the ability to record new micro-samples by the user, making it more accurately a *rompler*, rather than a sampler.

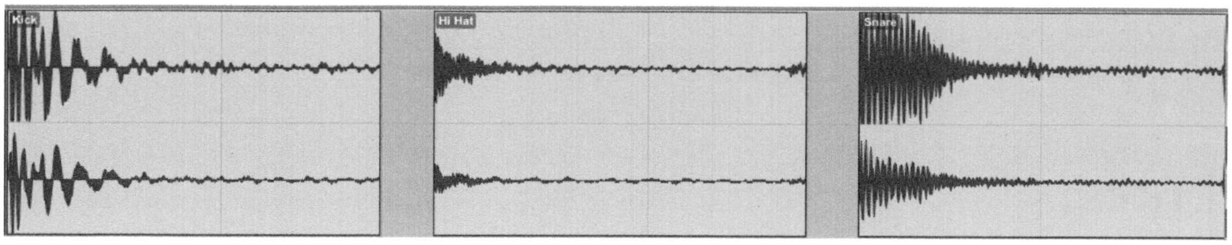

FIG. 4.1. A Kick Drum, Hi-Hat, and Snare Drum Micro-Sample

Enter the Akai S900 in 1986. This device changed how hip-hop music could and would be made. It was a more cost-effective product than the extremely expensive sampling devices that were on the scene at that time, such as the Fairlight and the Synclavier (used by producers) or the DMX 15-80 S and the Publison Infernal Machine (used by engineers).

The S900 was the first truly affordable modular MIDI sampler, using 12 bits, a 40 kHz sample rate, 750 KB of RAM that allowed for about 12 seconds of recording time, and a storage capacity up to 32 samples.

The Akai S950, introduced in 1988 with a 48 kHz sampling rate, was followed by the S1000, also in 1988, which was a 16-bit, 44.1 kHz *stereo sampler* with 16 voices and up to 32 MB of RAM.

Akai's MPC (discussed previously) was also introduced in 1988, as a 12-bit, 40 kHz sampler, built into a 99-track sequencer with MIDI In/Out/Thru capability. This device was basically the S900 with a dedicated sequencer and drum pad controller. The game was changed forever with this device. Keyboard controllers then had a rival that didn't demand knowledge of music theory to operate. A shifting of the musical mind had found its ultimate tool. The success of the MPC series of devices dominated hip-hop well into the modern DAW era of the twenty-first century, and is still going strong with newer versions of MPCs.

The early MPCs had various iterations where the bit depth increased from 12 bits to 16 bits to 24 bits, each one with a better and better audio resolution. But the MPC loved by most beat makers was the MPC3000, released in 1994, which had a relatively low 16-bit resolution that resulted in a "gritty" sound. It seems that pristine audio is not a prerequisite for a "banging" beat. A little bit of grit is also necessary, and lower sampling rates provide that grit.

Another popular sampling sequencer of this period was the E-mu SP-1200, which debuted in 1987. It was an upgrade of the SP-12 drum sampler that had been introduced in 1985. The SP-1200 was a monophonic, 12-bit, 26.04 kHz sampling rate, MIDI In/Out/Thru sampler and sequencer. It stored patterns and songs differently than the MPC could, and its sound defined the early work of producers such as Pete Rock, Marley Marl, and Easy Mo Bee.

An interesting thing that hip-hop producers did with micro-samples was to leave a bit of the following hi-hat on kicks or snares. Playing this micro-sample at a different tempo would present the hi-hat in different swing positions other than the quantized position.

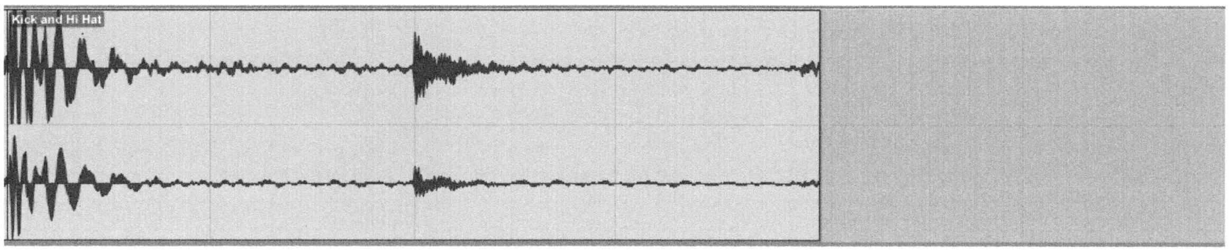

FIG. 4.2. A Kick Drum and Hi-Hat Micro-Sample

Another technique that hip-hop producers did with samplers was when they were recording audio from a turntable (instead of from tape, a microphone, or an instrument). In order to overcome the short 10-second sampling time available on these early devices, the producers would increase the speed on the turntable they were sampling from, which increased the tempo and raised the pitch, but shortened the length of the sound to be sampled. Once the short sample was captured, the pitch knob on the SP-1200 was used to decrease the tempo, lower the pitch, and lengthen the sample into a new piece of work with an embedded "grittiness" because of the compromised sampling process. This became the way to work with the SP-1200. Try it, if you dare....

Eventually, the MPC found a rival for hip-hop production and beat making. The Ensoniq ASR-10, released in 1992, was loved by quite a few hip-hop producers more than the MPC because it had a powerful onboard effects processor. In both a rack mount version and a 61-key "keyboard controller" version, the ASR-10 had an architecture more like a synthesizer than a sampler in the way it could modify recorded samples. It was a 16-bit, 30 kHz or 44.1 kHz sampling rate, 2 MB (expandable to 16 MB) 96 PPQN sampler/sequencer. This device was just grungy enough to have grit, but musically and technologically savvy enough to create a sound palette that set certain producers' beats apart from the crowd.

MACRO-SAMPLES

A *macro-sample* is a tempo-dependent sample that lasts for two or more beats. The macro-sample is inherently tied to tempo because of its longer duration than a micro- sample.

In the Golden Age of hip-hop (1987 to 1992), the typical length of recorded samples grew from four beats (one bar of 4/4), to two bars, to four bars and more due to expanded storage capacity by sampling manufacturers. No longer were the turntable and the vinyl disc going to be the source of looped four-bar drum patterns, because macro-sampling could sample any beat length and play it back with the simple push of a button. You could even layer in additional melodic, recorded performances.

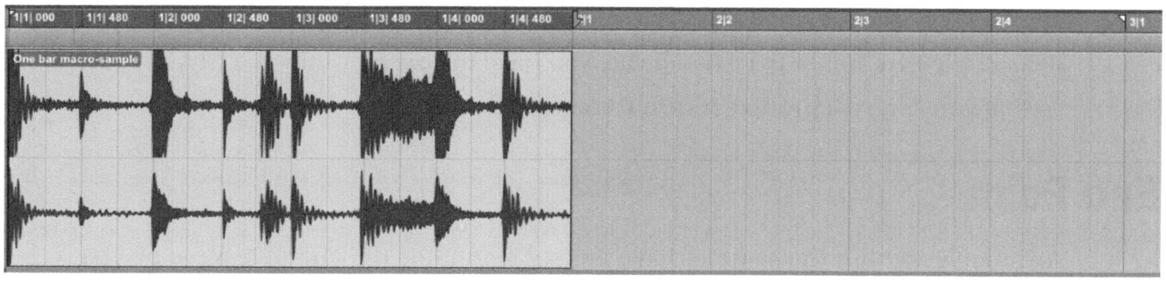

FIG. 4.3. A One-Bar Macro-Sample

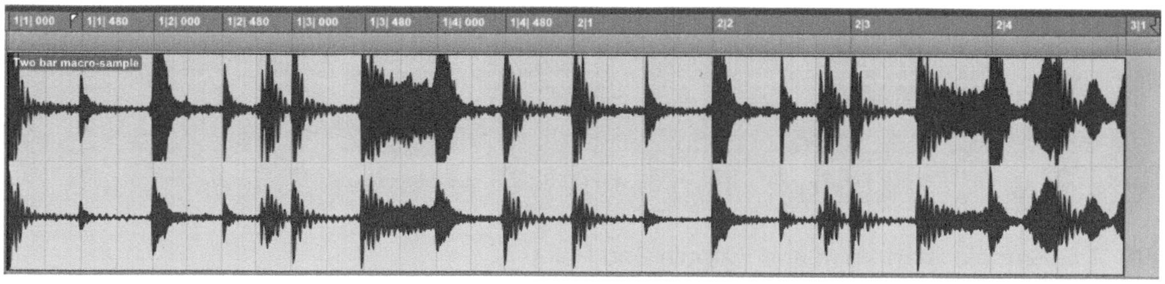

FIG. 4.4. A Two-Bar Macro-Sample

Long samples, recorded into a sampler, could then take on a more expressive creative dynamic aided by sample looping, sample sequencing, a powerful palate of MIDI commands, onboard dynamics processing, and time-based audio effects processing.

The macro-sample producer looks for those sections in old records that contain minimal to no vocal parts or a vocal part that is cool enough to withstand being listened to over and over. New lyrics and melodies are then superimposed over this beat, and the result is a new hit that contains the musical properties of an old hit.

Sampling is an art, and finding the right blend of old record to new idea is an essential part of the hip-hop beat maker's tool set.

SAMPLING FUNDAMENTALS

Manipulating a sampler has not changed much from 1987. To use a sampler, there are a few fundamental concepts you must understand before your beat making becomes effortless.

Start Point

All samples within the sampler have a *start point*. This is the beginning of the sample playback, but does not have to be the beginning of the recorded sample. It is the point used to line up the sample at a specific bar or beat within your composition. Micro-samples themselves range from short sounds—such as kick drum, snare, and percussion samples (like those used on the LinnDrum)—to more elongated and looped string, woodwind, and horn samples or orchestra hits. These short samples are simple to record and play back without affecting the timing of your song, but as the sample gets longer than two beats, you have to consider how the rhythm varies so that you can synchronize it with the song's tempo.

End Point

All samples within the sampler have an *end point*. It is the end of sample playback but does not have to be the end of the recorded sample.

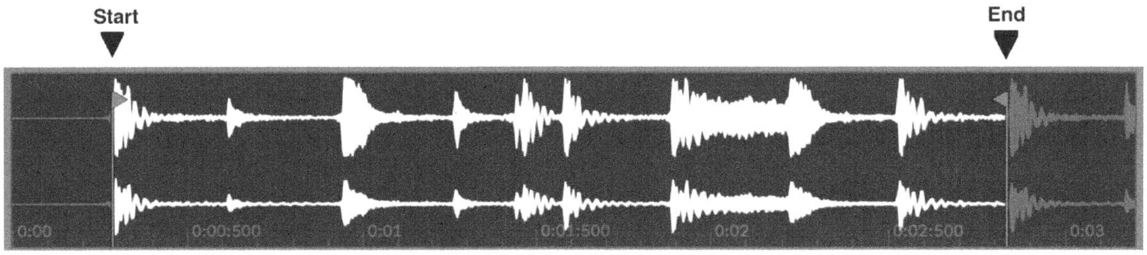

FIG. 4.5. Sample Start Point and Sample End Point

Pitch

Transposing the pitch of samples also affected the tempo, time, and length of a sample. The higher the pitch, the faster the tempo and shorter the sample; the lower the pitch the slower the tempo and longer the sample.

The formula used by turntables, analog tape machines, samplers, and DAW pitch engines is twelve-tone equal temperament, where each of the octaves above and below a known fundamental pitch is divided logarithmically into twelve steps. The ratio is equal to the twelfth root of two and is used to calculate the variation in semitones of pitch (Hz), the speed of your turntable (RPM), the speed of your tape machine (IPS), and the tempo of your song (bpm); and will contain an inverse relationship to the duration of time (HH:MM:SS:mm), length of tape (feet and inches), or the number of samples/second in your DAW.

The twelfth root of two, $\sqrt[12]{2}$, is the static number 1.05946309. When multiplied by itself 12 times, it equals 2, which, in the case of an octave, relates to the n^{12} ratio of pitch, turntable speed, tape speed, and tempo; and, in the inverse, the n^{-12} duration of time, length of a piece of analog tape or the number of samples.

The formula for chromatic intervals reads as follows:

$$f_n = f_0 \times (\sqrt[12]{2})^n$$

Since $\sqrt[12]{2}$ is a static number, it could also be written:

$$f_n = f_0 \times 1.05946309^n$$

Where:

- n is the chromatic variation from the known value
- 0 is the known value you are beginning with
- f is Hz, RPM (revolutions per minute), IPS (inches per second), or bpm (beats per minute); inverse n values are used for time (milliseconds or samples) and length (inches or centimeters).

Once again, and read it slowly so your eyes don't glaze over: as the known value of Hz (pitch), IPS, RPM, or bpm goes up, the pitch gets higher and the tempo of the music increases, but length and time (in your DAW, samples which are the smallest increment of time) decrease. And, as the known value of Hz, IPS, RPM, or bpm goes down, the pitch gets lower, the tempo decreases and the length and time (samples) increase.

Let's say I have a sample in the key of A minor and I want to change it to the key of C minor.

C is three chromatic increments above A 440 or nine increments below A 440.

So the pitch (f), which is 3 increments (n) above the pitch (f) that is known (440 Hz), multiplied by $\sqrt[12]{2}$ to the nth (in this case, 3rd) power equals 523.25 Hz.

Or, the pitch (f), which is –9 increments (n) below the pitch (f) that is known (440 Hz), multiplied by $\sqrt[12]{2}$ to the nth power (in this case, –9th) equals 261.62 Hz.

If I wanted to move the same A minor sample up three chromatic half-steps to C minor on a turntable spinning at 33.3 RPM:

$$f_3 = 33.3 \times (\sqrt[12]{2})^3 = 39.6 \text{ RPM}$$

If I wanted to move the same A minor sample up three chromatic half-steps to C minor on an analog tape machine moving at 30 IPS:

$$f_3 = 30 \times (\sqrt[12]{2})^3 = 35.67 \text{ IPS}$$

If that sample was playing at 120 bpm and I wanted to move it up three chromatic half steps to the key of C minor, what would the new tempo be?

$$f_3 = 120 \times (\sqrt[12]{2})^3 = 142.70 \text{ bpm}$$

If that A minor sample is a two-bar phrase at 120 bpm, its duration is 4 seconds. What would the new duration be if I changed it to C minor using this formula? (Remember, we are using negative n values now!)

$$f_{-3} = 4 \times (\sqrt[12]{2})^{-3} = 3.36 \text{ seconds}$$

If that A minor sample is a two-bar phrase at 120 bpm on an analog tape machine moving at 30 IPS, the length of the tape for that phrase would be 120 inches, or 10 feet. What would the new length be if I changed it to C minor using this formula?

$$f_{-3} = 120 \times (\sqrt[12]{2})^{-3} = 100.90 \text{ inches}$$

$$f_{-3} = 10 \times (\sqrt[12]{2})^{-3} = 8.40 \text{ feet}$$

If that A minor sample is a two-bar phrase at 120 bpm on a DAW session using a 48 kHz sampling rate, it would contain 192,000 samples. How many samples would it contain if I changed it to C minor using this formula?

$$f_{-3} = 192{,}000 \times (\sqrt[12]{2})^{-3} = 161{,}452 \text{ samples}$$

This concept of *equal temperament* is a mainstay of western music and is built in to the math of all our devices that handle pitch and time. Even though hip-hop beat makers might seem like they are pulling magic out of thin air, the devices they work with are adhering to physical principles that were worked out by French monk and mathematician Marin Mersenne in 1639. I'm sure there's a joke in there about Marin Mersenne being the long lost great-grandfather of hip-hop, but let me continue.

A major point of understanding that pitch alters tempo and duration, when it comes to manipulating samples in a sampler, is that editing macro-samples—especially in the early era of sampling—resulted in subtle pitch variations between two sections of the same song. Why? Most of the records sampled in this era were not metronomic. They had been performed by live musicians prior to the advent of the drum machine. If you sampled from the beginning of a song and then sampled another section from two minutes into the song, the two sections would probably be slightly out of time with each other. In order to get one in time with the other, you could alter the *pitch* parameter on the sampler to lengthen or shorten one of the samples relative to the other. This would also lower or raise the pitch of the sample.

From 1987 to 1992, there were a lot of records made with subtle pitch fluctuations from one section to another, which had the potential to interfere with any recorded overdubs from instruments or vocals.

One answer for this anomaly was that most beat makers in the Golden Age of hip-hop looked for samples that were extremely close in tempo to each other. You can hear it in the work of the Bomb Squad. Most of the samples chosen are pretty close to the original tempos of the songs they come from.

DEFAULT SAMPLING NOTE AND KEY RANGE

Sampling units usually default to recording the sample on middle C, or note number 60 in MIDI, which is known as C3. The sample can then be played down or up in pitch across the 128-note range, from C2 to G8. Hip-hop producers narrow the key range of samples so they can fit many samples into one sampling unit under one sampling *program*. The default sampling note can also be changed after the recording (or importing) of the sample.

Chopping

Beat makers, such as Pete Rock, would eventually adopt an editing concept called *chopping*, where they would slice a macro-sample into smaller pieces (e.g., eighth notes). By doing this, he could take a two-bar phrase and divide it into sixteen pieces. These smaller pieces could be triggered via MIDI in a sequencer in a quantized position that would line up with the tempo of the original whole piece. But now, each one of these pieces would have its own starting point on a separate note number of the sampler. Pete Rock would then change the tempo of the composition, and each piece would stay locked to its quantized position in the song. The tempo would now be different, but all the pitches would remain the same. This concept worked so well for him that eventually the Akai MPC sequencer adopted a function called slicing, which achieves the work of Pete Rock without the tedious chopping of the macro-sample. The descendants of this approach are tools like Quick Sampler in Logic Pro and Simpler in Ableton Live that contain beat, transient, and manual slicing.

Additional control—such as imposing the attack, decay, sustain, and release of envelope modifiers or LFO modifiers (lo-pass, hi-pass, band-pass, or notch filters) and parametric EQ—can affect the way a sample sounds and make it easier to combine with other instruments in your composition.

Looping

The difference between the sample of a percussive sound like a snare drum and the sample of a sustaining sound like a violin is that the violin needs to play for as long as you hold down the key on your controller. This function is provided by a feature called *looping*, which is contained in most samplers. When you play a sound, it plays to its conclusion, then loops back to a specified *loop start point*, and continues playing to a specified *loop end point*. As long as you hold down the key on the controller, it continues to loop around these two points. The result is an elongated sustain even though you have recorded a micro-sample.

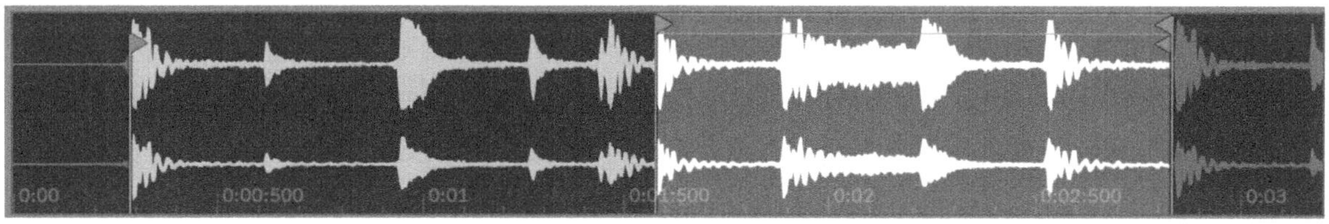

FIG. 4.6. One-Bar Phrase That Repeatedly Loops Back to Beat 2

Huge note: sample *looping* is not to be confused with sample *sequencing*. Almost all hip-hop records use sample sequencing (not looping) to "loop" a multi-bar phrase.

ACTIVITIES CHAPTER 4

Listening

Using your favorite playback app, listen to "It's My Thing" by Marva Whitney (1969) and "Get Off Your Ass and Jam" by Funkadelic (1975), which became "Bring the Noise" by Public Enemy (1988); "Funky Drummer" by James Brown and the J.B.'s (1970) and "It's My Thing" by Marva Whitney (1969), which became "F*** tha Police" by N.W.A (1989); "Alone Again (Naturally)" by Gilbert O'Sullivan (1971) and "Impeach the President" by the Honey Drippers (1973), which became "Alone Again" by Biz Markie (1991).

Make note of the stereo imaging (things on the left and right), instrument choices, and tempos. What are the similarities and differences between these compositions? What are the similarities and differences between these compositions and the compositions from the previous chapter?

Can you identify the specific songs and sections of those songs that were sampled to make the final compositions? When you feel that you have sufficiently analyzed these compositions, move on to the production exercises for this chapter.

Production

Download

DAW Track 4.1 PC The Power

Access the practice files for these activities via the link and code on the first page of this book.

1. **Listen to the beat.** Import the stereo mix of "PC The Power" to your DAW. Listen for the layered samples, and list the phrases that you believe are samples.
2. **Rap to the beat.** Import the stereo mix of "PC The Power to your DAW. Rap the lyrics of "Fight The Power" recorded on a separate track.
3. **Rap to the separated files of the beat.** Import the individual files to have control over each sound. Rap the lyrics of "Fight The Power" on a separate track. Mix to taste.
4. **Create your own beat.** Use the virtual instruments in your DAW to create your own beat and rap that sounds like the sampling era in hip-hop.

PART II

Hip-Hop Regional Variations

The story of hip-hop is that it was birthed in the Bronx. This is true! But, the brothers, sisters, visiting cousins, extended family, and friends of the originators (who came to visit during summers and holidays) brought news of the cultural phenomenon back to their hometowns. It was not long before hip-hop took on the flavor of the west coast, the south, and the Midwest. This section outlines how the tools used for creating a recorded hip-hop changed across America's different geographic regions.

CHAPTER 5

East Coast Hip-Hop: Micro-Sampling

LISTENING: EAST COAST HIP-HOP

- "White Lines" by Grandmaster Flash and Melle Mel (1984)
- "Jam On It" by Newcleus (1984)
- "Roxanne, Roxanne" by U.T.F.O. (1984)
- "Walk This Way" by Run DMC (1985)
- "Rebel Without a Pause" by Public Enemy (1987)

The period from 1979 to 1987 birthed our digital music age, and it birthed hip-hop. The very idea of what was needed to create music changed radically. For many, the first impression of hip-hop was that music was being stolen and rigor was being abandoned. The sheer force of will it takes to learn an instrument or coax complex melodies out of your voice seemed to be missing in the hip-hop genre. It was simultaneously musical, but not "music," as defined by musicians and musical institutions. To this day, music education is still trying to come to terms with the instructional language that complements hip-hop proficiency.

What we do know is that *breakdancing, DJ'ing, MC'ing,* and *graffiti* are the four foundational cornerstones of hip-hop. And, in retrospect, the housing projects of east coast urban neighborhoods were a fertile ground for this new youth movement, partly because cramped living quarters and encroaching urban development schemes demanded that entertainment occur in smaller and smaller spaces. Live bands in clubs gave way to turntables, which gave way to live bands in studios, which gave way to drum machines and synthesizers, which gave way to MIDI and sequencers, which gave way to samplers, all the while cutting the cost of production, and the physical space needed to create, at each step. Hip-hop came of age on the east coast and finally crossed over to pop acceptance in 1985 with the Run DMC hit "Walk This Way."

Although the Sedgwick Housing Projects in the Bronx is ground zero, and DJ Kool Herc was the guy who lit the fuse that traveled around the world, the Northeast Corridor (which includes Boston, New York, New Jersey, and Philadelphia) contributed to the early expansion of hip-hop. The rappers from "Rapper's Delight" all hailed from Englewood, New Jersey. The producer of "Planet Rock," Arthur Baker, was from Boston, Massachusetts. Rapper Schoolly D, who wrote and produced "P.S.K. What Does It Mean" (1985) and was considered by rapper Ice-T to be the first gansta rapper, hailed from Philadelphia, Pennsylvania.

While it may be logical to describe a hip-hop producer as someone who uses musical tools to achieve a listenable product, that is not the complete picture at all. There is also a thought process, and in many cases, that thought process would purposefully reflect regional differences. Similar to the Kansas City sound in jazz, the Detroit sound in soul, or the Nashville sound in country, hip-hop eventually began to display similar sorts of regional variations.

ELEMENTS OF HIP-HOP STYLES

Let's explore some specific ways to vary hip-hop compositions and how preferences for these elements of shaped the variations in hip-hop that we will discuss throughout this book. We'll begin with identifying characteristics of east coast hip-hop.

TEMPO

One of the first things to consider when you sit down to make a beat is the tempo. The tempo will help you to determine the fit of the musical aspects you will add. The average tempo of a typical east coast composition from the old school (1979–86) was between 100 and 120 bpm. This speed seemed to work equally well for dancing and rapping.

Track	Tempo
"Rockit" by Herbie Hancock (1982)	110 bpm
"Hip-Hop, Be Bop (Don't Stop)" by Man Parish (1982)	120 bpm
"White Lines (Don't Do It)" by Melle Mel (1983)	115 bpm
"It's Yours" by T La Rock (1983)	100 bpm
"It's Like That" by Run DMC (1983)	120 bpm

FIG. 5.1. Tempos of East Coast Hits

A long list of notable east coast hip-hop artists such as Eric B & Rakim, Kool Moe Dee, and Slick Rick have a body of work within 100 bpm to 120 bpm. Succeeding generations of east coast artists even up to the present have honored this old school tempo preference as true to the east coast aesthetic within hip-hop.

INSTRUMENTATION

Old-school hip-hop record production began with live bands being recorded to emulate the DJ'ing techniques coming out of urban projects. A full drum kit, electric bass, electric guitar, acoustic or electric piano, synthesizer, and turntable could create a great beat in 1979 or 1980, but as digital technology took hold, the way people created and the way people received the music shifted, and the sound of a live band began to sound dated, unless it was sampled from a record.

Beat-making preferences began to lean towards instruments like the TR-808, whose hi-hat, cowbell, and rim shot sounds are truly unique and easy to differentiate from other drum machines, and the DMX, with an equally unique library that sounded much more like actual drum sounds.

Almost all bass lines in east coast hip-hop, post the live band era, were either played on synthesizers or derived from samples. Synthesizers were also used to fill out compositions as replacements for guitars, keyboards, strings, and horns, in melodic fashion or to punctuate chords.

The turntable skills of good DJs showed up in the recording studio primarily as scratches that were used to add rhythmic pushes to songs, instead of tom-toms. Since a drum machine is static and metronomic, a good scratch artist can add a sense of the human feel back into the composition with well-placed vinyl manipulation.

Rounding out east coast instrumentation, using samplers provides almost limitless musical creativity. From a micro-sampled kick to a macro-sampled guitar, keyboard, horn, or string figure—or even a sample of a DJ's scratch performance—the sampler makes it harder and harder to listen to a recording and know definitively whether you are listening to an original performance or a sampled performance. East coast hip-hop is known for its use of sampling in an interpolative, collage-like fashion.

RHYTHMIC FEEL

There was a lot of experimentation going in early east coast hip-hop, but even with that, many of the compositions were designed with a similar goal in mind, and that was to make people dance.

Kick-drum patterns would move playfully but usually commit to a solid hit on the first beat of a one- or two-bar phrase. Hi-hat performances would follow an eighth- or sixteenth-note pattern (with a slightly lazy swing), which would establish much of the movement in the song. Snares, rim shots, and claps shared the backbeat on the second and fourth beats, with periodic punctuation similar to tom-toms in soul and funk music.

Vocal and hi-hat rhythms actually helped to define the east coast sound, and are two of the primary instruments that producers from other regions began to change as a reflection of their regional tastes.

Rhythms in hip-hop did not stay confined to rigid quantization. Some beat makers were trying to make beats without turntables or drum kits. They would create their beats using multiple tape machines and the stop/record/play buttons. The result was an irregular, interesting timing that eventually producers such as J Dilla would emulate with a sampler instead.

SONIC DENSITY

Sonic density indicates how clearly individual instruments can be heard in a record relative to other instruments, including the vocals.

In the first few years of hip-hop production, the sonic density of hip-hop recordings shifted quickly. If you listen to the live band era, you will be able to discern each of the conventional instruments, and the vocals, clearly.

In the drum machine/sequencer era you will hear a much more sparse production that has a few drum elements, a few synthesizer elements and prominent vocals.

The sampling era brought forward a more dense and complex arrangement of micro- and macro-samples. Even though equalizers are usually used to reduce or boost the frequencies of one instrument relative to another instrument, a single sample can have an entire band or orchestra embedded, and that makes the job of equalizing samples more difficult but very satisfying when done well.

MICRO-SAMPLING

The debut of the Linn LM-1 in 1980 began the era of the micro-sample in hip-hop. Short-duration kicks, snares, hi-hats, toms, and crashes rapidly became the hip-hop sound of the 1980s. The debut of the S900 sampler in 1987 completed the technological journey of east coast hip-hop and micro-sampling began giving way to macro-sampling, and both east coast and west coast producers began to reflect the shift towards longer and longer musical samples.

ACTIVITIES CHAPTER 5

Listening

Using your favorite playback app, listen to "White Lines" by Grandmaster Flash and Melle Mel (1984), "Jam On It" by Newcleus (1984), "Roxanne, Roxanne" by U.T.F.O. (1984), "Walk This Way" by Run DMC (1985), "Rebel Without a Pause" by Public Enemy (1987).

Make note of the tempo, instrumentation, rhythmic feel and sonic density. What are the similarities and differences between these compositions? Can you identify the micro-samples in these compositions? Are there modern compositions that sound like they are influenced by this early east coast aesthetic? If so, where are those producers from?

Production Exercise

Create your own beat. Use the virtual instruments in your DAW to create a beat and rap that sounds like one of the early east coast eras in hip-hop. If you have not created your own beats in production exercises 1 through 4, now is the opportunity to explore your creative potential. If you have created your own beats in production exercises 1 through 4, use this production exercise to become even better at east-coast beat making by creating sound-alikes for all the compositions listed in chapters 1 through 4.

CHAPTER 6

West Coast Hip-Hop: Technological Hybrid

LISTENING: WEST COAST HIP-HOP

- "Mothership Connection" by Parliament (1975)
- "Let Me Ride" by Dr. Dre (1992)
- "Atomic Dog" by George Clinton (1982)
- "Who Am I (What's My Name)" by Snoop Dogg (1993)

Hybrid music production skills—the blending of turnatablism, live band production, drum machine/synthesis, MIDI/sequencing, and sampling—show up prominently in the production sound of the west coast. While hip-hop was birthed in New York, and the east coast is considered the initial regional version of hip-hop, innovative creativity soon spread beyond the northeast corridor. In California, N.W.A (Ni**az Wit Attitudes, a group that rivaled the political urgency of Public Enemy) used the Bomb Squad micro- and macro-sampling formula to come up with their critique of law enforcement titled "F*** tha Police" (1988). Over the next few years, west coast beat making would eventually push beyond the conventions of east coast beat making. In their quests for a unique west coast sound, the search yielded a funk-infused hybrid of drum machines (using micro-samples), samplers (using macro-samples), real musicians (using conventional live band recording techniques), and MIDI/music sequencing. One of the first differentiating factors used by west coast beat makers was to perform their compositions at slower tempos than those by their east coast counterparts.

Instead of using soul and early funk samples of artists such as James Brown, beat makers like Dr. Dre dug deeper into the musical style that succeeded early funk. When James Brown's band quit in the early 1970s, George Clinton (the leader of Parliament-Funkadelic) picked up Brown's entourage and charged them with creating a newer, psychedelic form of funk called *p-funk*.

Similar to how the east coast had James Brown as its iconic figure, the west used George Clinton and Parliament Funkadelic as their north star. It worked, and west coast hip-hop, which had already been grabbing dominance of the charts from the east coast for a few years (since the debut of "F*** tha Police") cemented its own voice with a sound that was no longer reminiscent of the east coast.

When Dr. Dre released *The Chronic* in 1992 he came up with a twist on the blending of turntables, live band production, drum machines, synthesizers, MIDI, music sequencing, and sampling, called *g-funk* (gangsta funk), based on the synthesizer driven p-funk sound of Parliament-Funkadelic. Instead of tempos ranging between 100 and 120 bpm, Dr. Dre slowed his beats down to a range of 90 to 100 bpm. (Note: West Coast tempos range from 90 to 180 bpm, but *The Chronic* used this narrower range of tempos to define G-Funk.) The slower tempos allowed the dialect of west coast rappers a more comfortable bed for their articulation. It's a warmer, slower, more sprawling lifestyle on the west coast, so why not have beats that reflect the rhythm of that warmer, slower culture? And it wasn't only Parliament-Funkadelic that Dre sampled; a wide landscape of black recording artists showed up in his work—even artists such as comedian Rudy Ray Moore.

Now, I'm not saying there wasn't a vibrant hip-hop scene on the west coast prior to Dr. Dre, because there was. Many would say that it ran concurrent to the east coast incubator period, the old school. Artists such as Uncle Jamm's Army, Mix Master Spade, and Egyptian Lover rose to prominence on local radio and within the performance venues of their communities, in much the same way that it was occurring on the east coast. But the national charts didn't have room for all this hip-hop at one time, so it took a while for the west coast to finally emerge as a dominant player in hip-hop on a national scale.

"F*** tha Police" was the successful and controversial record that showcased west coast hip-hop. The record's elements were based on an aesthetic that had already worked on the east coast. As a matter of fact, the same horn sample from Marva Whitney's "It's My Thing" that was used in "Fight the Power" by Public Enemy (1987) is prominently featured in "F*** tha Police." The first time I heard it, I actually thought the Bomb Squad had produced the record, but it is credited to Dr. Dre and DJ Yella.

Ice-T weighs in during this period of west coast development with a heavy metal band and an album called *Body Count* (1991), which in line with records such as "Walk This Way," proffered the idea that rock and rap could coexist.

In 1990, a consortium of artists that included Tone Loc, Young MC, MC Hammer, Ice-T, and Dr. Dre showed up on a single called "We're All in the Same Gang." While all these artists contributed to the development of the west coast scene, the musical approach of their combined effort was still a mirror of the beat making styles of the east coast.

Although the west coast has had many artists and beat makers, for me, west coast efforts like "Let Me Ride" by Dr. Dre (1992) and "Who Am I (What's My Name)" by Snoop Dogg (1993), are the sound that pushed hip-hop from the *soul-inspired*, 1960s-influenced beats of the east coast into a more modern *funk-inspired*, 1970s-influenced beat. The result, while still as interpolative as an east coast beat, gave the west coast its own separate and unique identity.

TEMPO

West coast hip-hop tempos range from 100 to 120 bpm, but prior to the release of *The Chronic* by Dr. Dre (1992), the west coast was replicating the east coast's 100–120 range of tempos, with an occasional outlier, like MC Hammer's "U Can't Touch This" (1990) or Yo-Yo's "You Can't Play With Me" (1991).

Track	Tempo (bpm)
"U Can't Touch This" by MC Hammer (1990)	130
"Funky Cold Medina" by Tone Loc (1989)	118
"Bust a Move" by Young MC (1989)	116
"The Humpty Dance" by Digital Underground (1990)	104
"You Can't Play with My Yo-Yo" by Yo-Yo (ft. Ice Cube, 1991)	96

FIG. 6.1. Tempos of West Coast Hip-Hop Hits Prior to the Release of *The Chronic*

On *The Chronic* most of the songs were within a 90 to 95 bpm range, with a few slower outliers.

Track	Tempo (bpm)
The Chronic (Intro)	89.2
F*** Wit Dre Day (And Everybody's Celebratin') [ft. Snoop Dogg, Jewell & RBX]	93.5
Let Me Ride (ft. Jewell)	92.3
The Day the Ni**az Took Over (ft. Daz, Snoop Dogg & RBX)	93.7
Nuthin' but a G Thang (ft. Snoop Dogg)	94.5
Deeez Nuuuts (ft. Dat Ni**a Daz, Nate Dogg, Snoop Dogg & Warren G)	93.5
Lil' Ghetto Boy (ft. Daz & Snoop Dogg)	92.2
A Ni**a Witta Gun (ft. Snoop Dogg)	87.5
Rat-Tat-Tat-Tat (ft. BJ "Tha Mocking Bird," Snoop Dogg & RBX)	86.1
The $20 Sack Pyramid (ft. Snoop Dogg, Big T*tt*e Nickie & Samara)	87.1
Lyrical Gangbang (ft. Kurupt, RBX & Rage)	81.0
High Powered (ft. Dat Ni**a Daz, RBX & Rage)	76.0
The Doctor's Office (ft. Jewell, Rage & Kevin Lewis)	75.5
Stranded on Death Row (ft. Bushwhack Bill, Snoop Dogg, Kurupt, RBX & Rage)	91.3
The Roach (The Chronic Outro) [ft. Dat Ni**a Daz, Emmage, Jewell, RBX & Rage]	89.2
B*tch*s Ain't Sh*t (ft. Dat Ni**a Daz, Snoop Dogg & Kurupt)	92.2

FIG. 6.2. Tempos on *The Chronic*

The album *Doggystyle* by Snoop Dogg (aka Snoop Doggy Dogg), produced by Dr. Dre, was released in 1993 and continued the g-funk production sound that Dre had captured on *The Chronic. Doggystyle* showcased its compositions within a 90 to 100 bpm range, with even fewer outliers.

Track	Tempo (bpm)
Bathtub	83.3
G Funk Intro	100.0
Gin and Juice (ft. Dat Ni**a Daz)	94.6
Tha Shiznit	96.8
Lodi Dodi (ft. Nancy Fletcher)	78.1
Murder Was the Case (Death After Visualizing Eternity)	90.5
Serial Killa (ft. The D.O.C., Tha Dogg Pound & RBX)	99.5
Who Am I (What's My Name)	96.8
For All My Ni**az & B*tch*s	88.1
Ain't No Fun (If the Homies Can't Have None)	100.1
Doggy Dogg World (ft. The Dramatics & Tha Dogg Pound)	94.3
GZ and Hustlas (ft. Nancy Fletcher)	91.3
Pump Pump	97.2

FIG. 6.3. Tempos on *Doggystyle*

INSTRUMENTATION

Samples reigned supreme in the west coast hip-hop sound of this period. From the interpolation of Rick James' "Super Freak" (1981) in MC Hammer's "U Can't Touch This" (1990) to the interpolation of Leon Haywood's "I Want'a Do Something Freaky to You" (1975) in Dr. Dre's "Nuthin' But a G Thang" (1992), sampling was a key that unlocked the purse strings of an ever-growing hip-hop audience. "Nuthin' But a G Thang" scored a coup, rising to No. 2 on the Billboard Hot 100 charts.

A focus for our production concerns, however, are the instrumental choices and melodic vocal inspirations on Dr. Dre's "Let Me Ride" and Snoop Dogg's "Who Am I (What's My Name)." The samples in these records have been organized with the MPC and augmented with digital kicks, snares, and hi-hats, like much of Dr. Dre's work. But, the vocal interpolations, which were lifted directly from

Parliament-Funkadelic compositions, are of particular note because they reinvigorated an interest in Parliament-Funkadelic—and probably all the funk bands of the 1970s—for a younger generation.

The MPC sampler/sequencer emerged from this period as the clear winner, in terms of tools used to create a west coast composition.

RHYTHMIC FEEL

Dr. Dre incorporated the swing feature of the MPC sampler/sequencer on "Let Me Ride" by using a shuffle feel. Let me briefly explain. The 96 PPQN (pulse per quarter note) resolution of an MPC60 (1988) splits a quarter note into quantized sixteenth-note durations of 24 pulses each. When you apply swing to a sixteenth-note figure, the second and fourth sixteenth notes of the figure are delayed by a few pulses. This swing was later incorporated into most DAWs as a preset with the designations such as Logic Swing A, B, C, D, E, and F, with each level successively delaying beats 2 and 4 by another two pulses.

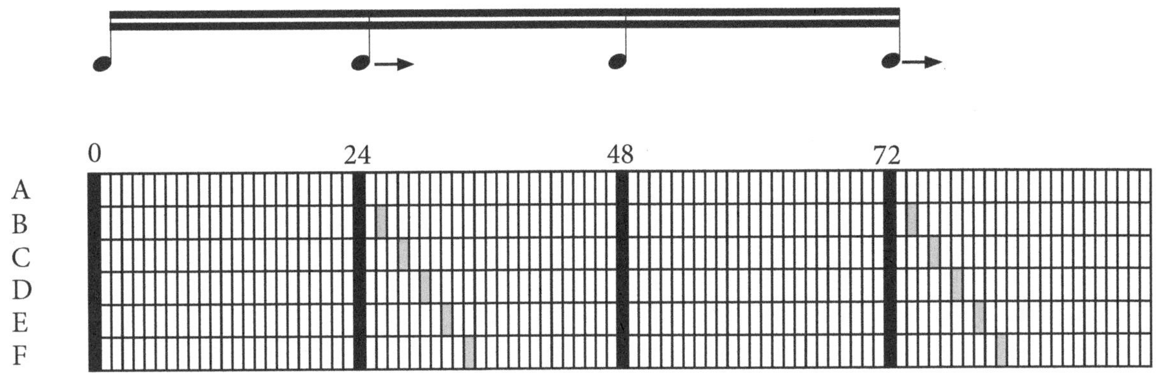

FIG. 6.4. Sixteenth-Note Swing Variations

Swing A is straight sixteenth-note quantization where the four subdivisions of a sixteenth-note figure (1 e & a) break up the 96 pulse as follows: 0, 24, 48, 72, where 0 is the downbeat (1), 24 is the second sixteenth (e), 48 is the upbeat (&), and 72 is the fourth sixteenth (a).

The way a four-bar pattern looks numerically, such as in the MPC's step edit page, is:

SWING A	**Subdivisions of Each Beat**			
	First	**Second**	**Third**	**Fourth**
One Measure	Beat 1.00	**1.24**	1.48	**1.72**
	Beat 2.00	**2.24**	2.48	**2.72**
	Beat 3.00	**3.24**	3.48	**3.72**
	Beat 4.00	**4.24**	4.48	**4.72**

Swing B adds two increments to the second and fourth sixteenth notes. The result looks like this.

SWING B	Subdivisions of Each Beat			
	First ♪	Second ♪	Third ♪	Fourth ♪
One Measure	Beat 1.00	**1.26**	1.48	**1.74**
	Beat 2.00	**2.26**	2.48	**2.74**
	Beat 3.00	**3.26**	3.48	**3.74**
	Beat 4.00	**4.26**	4.48	**4.74**

Notice how the first and third notes of the sixteenth-note pattern are still the same? This will stay constant throughout the rest of these swing patterns.

Swing C adds two more increments to the second and fourth sixteenth notes.

SWING C	Subdivisions of Each Beat			
	First ♪	Second ♪	Third ♪	Fourth ♪
One Measure	Beat 1.00	**1.28**	1.48	**1.76**
	Beat 2.00	**2.28**	2.48	**2.76**
	Beat 3.00	**3.28**	3.48	**3.76**
	Beat 4.00	**4.28**	4.48	**4.76**

Swing D adds two more increments to the second and fourth sixteenth notes.

SWING D	Subdivisions of Each Beat			
	First ♪	Second ♪	Third ♪	Fourth ♪
One Measure	Beat 1.00	**1.30**	1.48	**1.78**
	Beat 2.00	**2.30**	2.48	**2.78**
	Beat 3.00	**3.30**	3.48	**3.78**
	Beat 4.00	**4.30**	4.48	**4.78**

Swing E adds two more increments to the second and fourth sixteenth notes. This is the location of a pure triplet; if you subdivide 96 by 3, you get 32. Look at the number, after the decimal, in the second and fourth subdivisions.

SWING E	Subdivisions of Each Beat			
	First ♩ (3)	Second ♪ (3)	Third ♩ (3)	Fourth ♪ (3)
One Measure	Beat 1.00	**1.32**	1.48	**1.80**
	Beat 2.00	**2.32**	2.48	**2.80**
	Beat 3.00	**3.32**	3.48	**3.80**
	Beat 4.00	**4.32**	4.48	**4.80**

Swing F swing adds two more increments to the second and fourth subdivisions. This is later than a pure triplet and gives the illusion of a "push" into the next downbeat—sort of like a samba rhythm.

SWING F	Subdivisions of Each Beat			
	First	Second	Third	Fourth
One Measure	Beat 1.00	**1.34**	1.48	**1.82**
	Beat 2.00	**2.34**	2.48	**2.82**
	Beat 3.00	**3.34**	3.48	**3.82**
	Beat 4.00	**4.34**	4.48	**4.82**

You can hear the slight drag of a B swing on the hi-hat figure of Dr. Dre's "Let Me Ride" (1993), which uses a loop of sampled drums from "Kissing My Love" (1972) by Bill Withers. There are a few songs on that album that shuffle the sixteenth notes using the swing parameter, which can be done with a swing knob on an MPC or edited in with MIDI data on DAWs.

The MPC's swing knob has a second and fourth note variation, in 1% increments, from 50% to 75%. The 50% setting is the equivalent of Swing A and 66% is the equivalent of Swing E.

The other rhythmic variation that is characteristic of the sound of west coast hip-hop is triplets used by rappers. In the first verse of "Who Am I (What's My Name)," Snoop Dogg raps, "Follow me, follow me, follow me, follow me." The rhythm of this phrase is sixteenth-note triplets, and although this is not the first time this rhythmic figure appears on record, it is one of the most iconic early versions of sixteenth-note triplets recorded in west coast hip-hop.

SONIC DENSITY

The sonic density of a g-funk record is primarily based on the sample, or samples, chosen for interpolation. New hi-hats, snares, and kicks are added to beef up the sonic image, resulting in a more hi-fidelity version of the interpolated composition. This kind of additional layering occurs on "Let Me Ride," where lead synth melodies and string synth melodies also punctuate the composition.

If a part couldn't be sampled in a way that the producer or beat maker wanted to use it in the composition, a musician would be called in to perform the instrument live. The best portion of the performance would then be sampled into an MPC sampler/sequencer and played back into the composition with a more cyclically consistent arrangement.

The west coast was also rising at the same time that playback technology was seeing huge transformations. CD sales eclipsed vinyl in 1988 and surpassed cassette tapes by 1992. Music encoded as digital data did not have the same frequency restrictions as vinyl pressings, and this gave hip-hop producers the ability to expand the frequency response of their recordings by turning the low frequencies up louder in their records than the low frequencies in the records of other genres.

TECHNOLOGICAL HYBRID

The entry of g-funk in 1992 is a clear point of differentiation from the sound of east coast hip-hop. Where the east coast gravitated towards each new technology almost to the exclusion of previous technologies, the west coast hybridized turntablism, the live band, drum machine, synthesizers, MIDI, music sequencing and sampling all under one umbrella. Add to that differences in tempo, rhythmic feel, and sonic density, and you have the first radical expansion of hip-hop beat making and production skills.

ACTIVITIES CHAPTER 6

Listening

Using your favorite playback app, listen to "Mothership Connection" by Parliament (1975), "Let Me Ride" by Dr. Dre (1992), "Atomic Dog" by George Clinton (1982), and "Who Am I (What's My Name)" by Snoop Dogg (1993). Make note of the tempo, instrumentation, rhythmic feel and sonic density. What are the similarities and differences between these compositions? Can you identify the micro- or macro-samples in these compositions? Are there modern compositions that sound like they are influenced by this early west coast aesthetic? If so, where are those producers from? When you feel that you have sufficiently analyzed these compositions, move on to the production exercises for this chapter.

Production

Download

DAW Track 6.1 PC's My Name

Access the practice files for these activities via the link and code on the first page of this book.

1. **Listen to the beat.** Import the stereo mix of "PC's My Name" to your DAW. Listen for the live performances, drum machine, synthesizers, and samples. List the drum tones (808, 909, etc.), synthesizer waveforms, and length of samples (in beats).
2. **Rap to the beat.** Import the stereo mix of "PC's My Name" to your DAW. Rap the lyrics of "Who Am I (What's My Name)," recorded on a separate track.
3. **Rap to the separated files of the beat.** Import the individual files to have control over each sound. Rap the lyrics of "Who Am I (What's My Name)" on a separate track. Mix to taste.
4. **Create your own beat.** Use the virtual instruments in your DAW to create your own beat and rap that sounds like the west coast era in hip-hop.

CHAPTER 7

East Coast Renaissance: Macro-Sampling

Listening: East Coast Renaissance

- "Juicy Fruit" by Mtume (1983), which became
- **"Juicy" by the Notorious B.I.G. (1994)**
- "Every Breath You Take" by the Police (1983), which became
- **"I'll Be Missing You" by Puff Daddy and the Family (1997)**

Although Russell Simmons' Def Jam Records, in NYC, was the acknowledged home of hip-hop icons Run DMC, LL Cool J, and Public Enemy, L.A.'s Death Row Records grabbed the focus of hip-hop in 1992 with the debut of Dr. Dre's *The Chronic.* West coast hip-hop continued its chart dominance throughout the next few years, but the east coast began a comeback due to the efforts of a fledgling company that took off like a wildfire. A young man inspired by the entrepreneurial spirit of Russell Simmons and his Def Jam record label heard the call for a return to glory for east coast hip-hop. That young man was Sean "Puffy" Combs, and his label was Bad Boy Records.

Bad Boy Records was formed in 1992 (officially incorporated in 1993) and had its first successful hip-hop recording with "Flava in Ya Ear" by Craig Mack (1994). The record was a party smash that had some interesting "industrial" sounding components built into its well-laid-out beat that was programmed using an E-mu SP-1200 sampler/sequencer. Def Jam records had been holding its own against the onslaught of west coast hits during the Golden Age of Hip-Hop, but the emergence of Bad Boy Records' assembly-line approach to making hits truly signaled that the east coast was back in the black.

TEMPO

East Coast Renaissance tempos have a range of 90 to 120 bpm, with the bulk of the compositions competing head to head with west coast hip-hop in the 90 to 100 bpm range. "Flava in Ya Ear" by Craig Mack (1994) clocked in at 90 bpm, "Juicy" by the Notorious B.I.G. (1994) was 96 bpm and "I'll Be Missing You" by Puff Daddy and The Family spun at 110 bpm.

INSTRUMENTATION

Many of this period's musical beds were created using audio loops within SP-1200 sampler/sequencers and MPC sampler/sequencers, augmented with strings, horns, drums, percussion, basses, keys, and digital guitars, from Roland, Yamaha, and Korg sound modules primarily. But almost all manufacturers whose products were affordable by hip-hop producers found their way into the recordings. Turntable scratches showed up less and less on east coast compositions during the Renaissance.

RHYTHMIC FEEL

Straight eighth notes and sixteenth notes are used in hi-hat figures and rap phrasing for East Coast Renaissance compositions. You can also detect a very slight swing in the phrasing of artists like Craig Mack and the Notorious B.I.G., which shows up as a slight "behind the beat" sort of rhyme flow.

SONIC DENSITY

It became harder and harder to tell which parts of sampled audio loops were augmented with supporting instrumentation because many of the hip-hop producers were pulling very good "church schooled" keyboard players into their recording sessions. Their task was to duplicate as many of the loops as they could by using MIDI. The MIDI performances would then work alongside the loops to expand the sonic body of the composition.

The challenge with most hip-hop samples that included more instrumentation than just drums was that the frequency range of the pianos, guitars, horns, or strings competed directly with the vocal performances. And, in a genre that is driven by what is being said as much as by what is being played behind it, the fine tuning of frequencies was usually something that big-budget recording engineers in big-budget studios had a better chance of pulling off. Many of the hip-hop producers during the Renaissance were working with budgets that could cover exorbitant sampling fees, exorbitant engineering fees, and exorbitant studio fees.

Hip-hop soul also benefitted from the success of rap-infused hip-hop. Dense gospel chord structures began to show up in the hip-hop soul work of the rest of the Bad Boy Records R&B roster. The beats used for artists like Mary J. Blige, Faith Evans, 112, and Total used the same technologies as rap records but emphasized singing as the driving force of the vocal messages. Multiple-note harmonies showed up in east and west coast compositions and even groups like Bone Thugs-n-Harmony, from the Midwest, shone during this period that saw rappers, singers, and the merging of the two, lighting up the charts with a national energy that rivaled the Motown era.

MACRO-SAMPLING

Long samples that are two, four, eight, or even sixteen bars in length are a noticeable trait in the East Coast Renaissance period. The skill of the producer was displayed not only in the ability to sample but also with the ingenuity of "what" to sample. The copyright infringement lawsuits that created a financial barrier for beat makers in the sampling era were now a badge of honor for the hugely successful East Coast Renaissance beat makers.

A great example is "Juicy" by the Notorious B.I.G. which used five samples from "Juicy Fruit (Fruity Instrumental Mix)." The keys intro comes from bars 51–59, the drum section comes from bars 59-63, the bass section comes from bars 65–69, the guitar section comes from bars 69–73, and the synths section comes from bars 73–81.

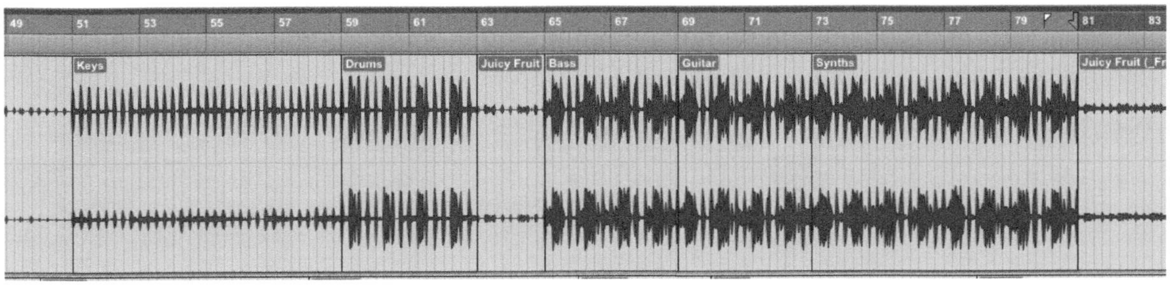

FIG. 7.1. The five sections of "Juicy Fruit (Fruity Instrumental Mix)" Sampled to Create "Juicy"

Those samples are then arranged in the MPC workstation's sequencer:

Keys Bars 1–9

Drums Bars 9–13

Bass Bars 13–21 (original four-bar section x 2)

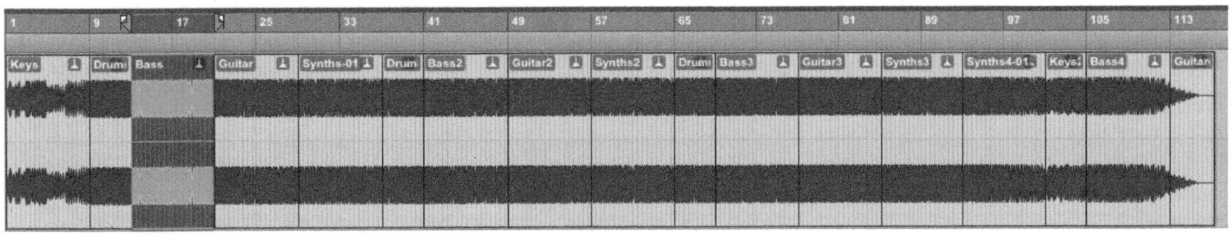

Guitar Bars 21–29 (original four-bar section x 2)

Synths Bars 29–37

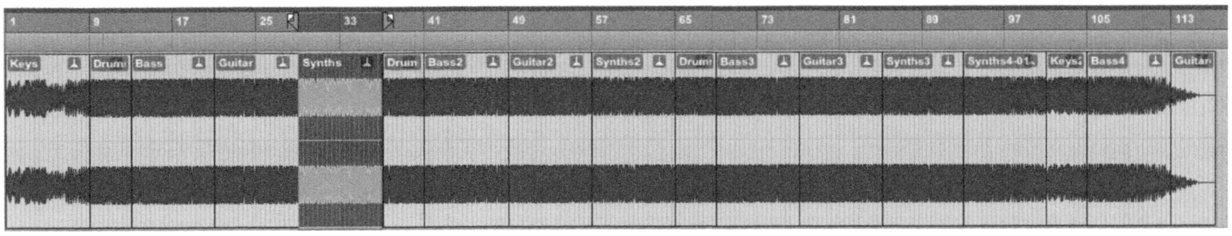

Drums Bars 37–41

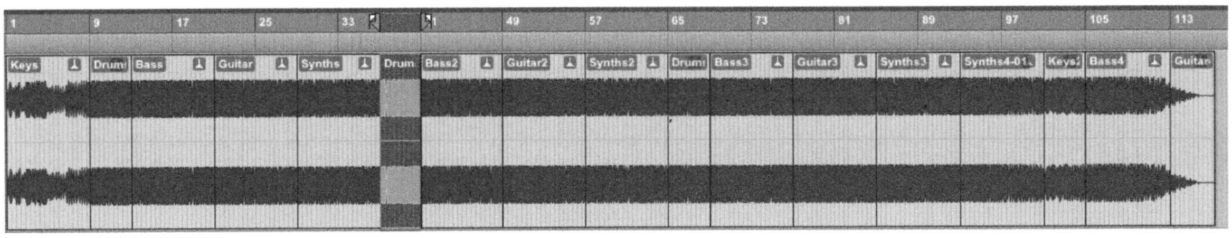

Bass Bars 41–49 (original four-bar section x 2)

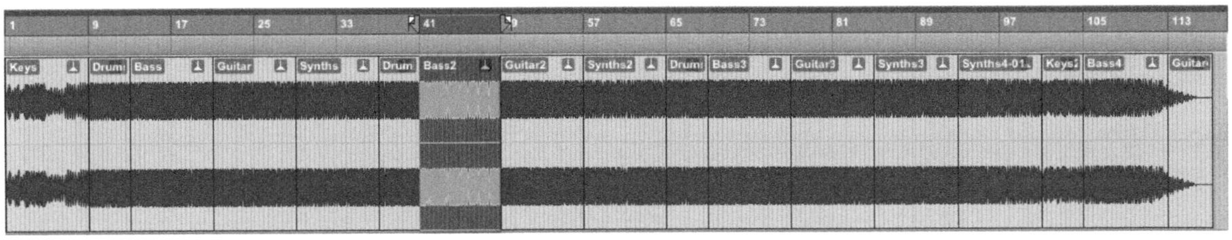

Guitar Bars 49–57 (original four-bar section x 2)

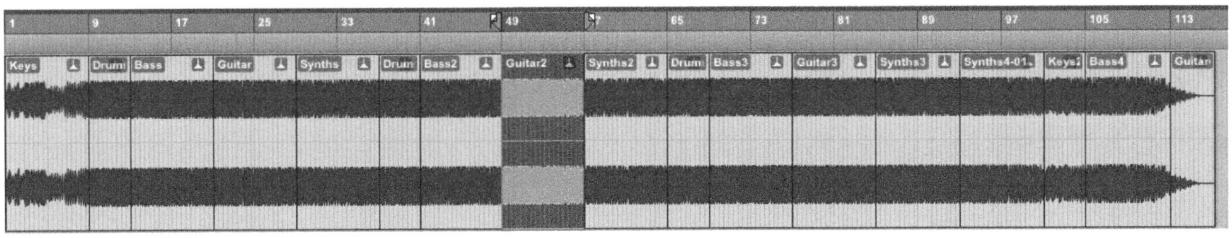

Synths Bars 57–65

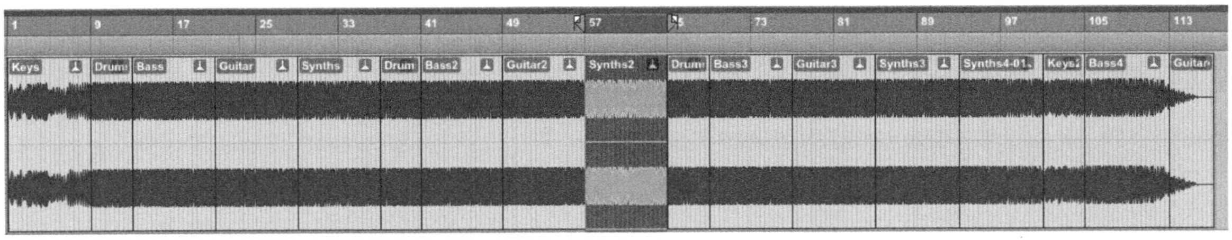

Drums Bars 65–69

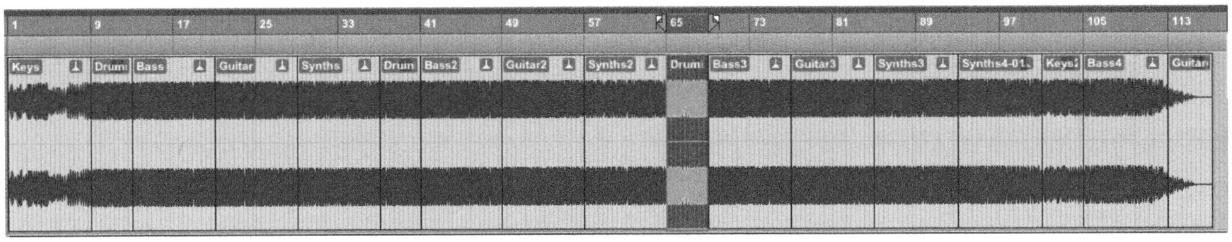

Bass Bars 69–77 (original four-bar section x 2)

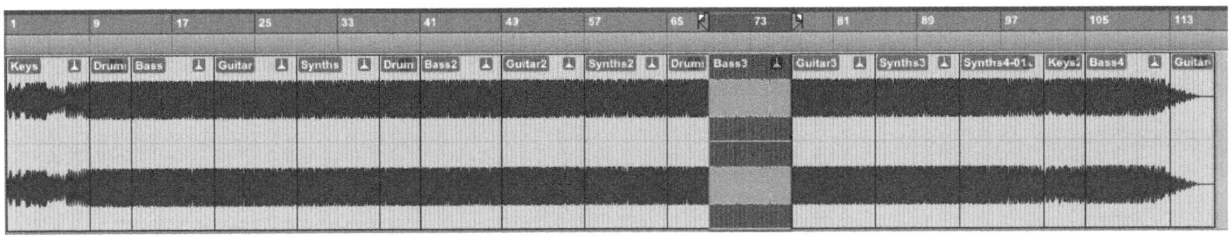

Guitar Bars 77–85 (original four-bar section x 2)

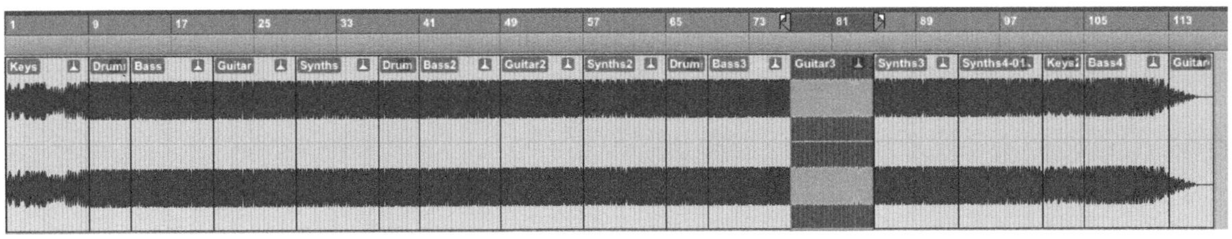

Synths Bars 85–93

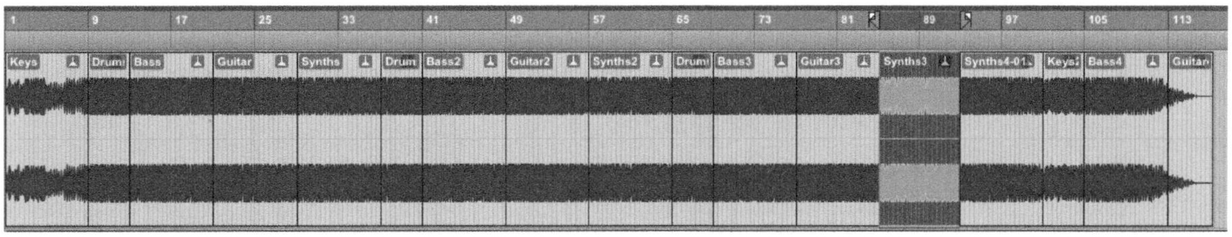

Synths Bars 93–101

Keys Bars 101–105 (half the original eight-bar section)

Bass Bars 105–113 (original four-bar section x 2)

Guitar Bars 133–Fade Out

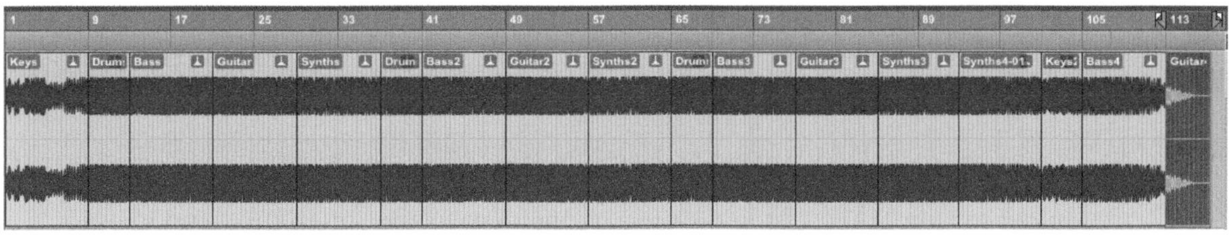

FIG. 7.2. Samples Used in "Juicy"

Successfully using samples from a previously recorded song was usually a sign that you had a large enough budget to afford the sampling fees. This flaunting of the ability to purchase sampling rights from the original authors became a badge of honor, or rather a badge of bling, for the artists that could afford to create this way. The battle for chart dominance through the mid 1990s was successfully waged by east coast beat makers using macro-samples.

But the battle between east and west coast beat makers and rappers turned into a full fledged war that would rage until the untimely deaths of hip-hop legends Tupac Shakur in 1996 and the Notorious B.I.G. in 1997.

Macro-sampling is still explored by successful hip-hop artists that can afford the sampling fees. Songs that have explored macro-sampling include "My House" by Flo Rida (2015) that sampled the very popular and often used "Impeach the President" by the Honey Drippers (1973), "I Like It" by Cardi B ft. Bad Bunny and J Balvin (2018) that sampled "I Like It Like That (A Mi Me usta Asi)" by Pete Rodriguez (1966), and "Future Bright" by Rick Ross ft. Bryson Tiller (2020) that sampled "Touch Me Tease Me" by Case ft. Foxy Brown and Mary J. Blige (1996).

Macro-sampling is still an important part of hip-hop beat making that easily traces its origin back to the the DJ skill of digging in the crates for that hot beat that moves the crowd.

ACTIVITIES CHAPTER 7

Listening

Using your favorite playback app, listen to "Juicy Fruit" by Mtume (1983), "Juicy" by the Notorious B.I.G. (1994), "Every Breath You Take" by the Police (1983), and "I'll Be Missing You" by Puff Daddy and the Family (1997). Make note of the tempo, instrumentation, rhythmic feel, and sonic density. What are the similarities and differences between these compositions? Can you identify the macro-samples in these compositions? Are there modern compositions that sound like they are influenced by this East Coast Renaissance aesthetic? If so, where are those producers from? When you feel that you have sufficiently analyzed these compositions, move on to the production exercises for this chapter.

Production

Download

DAW Track 7.1 PC's Juice

Access the practice files for these activities via the link and code on the first page of this book.

1. **Listen to the beat.** Import the stereo mix and the stereo macro- samples of "PC's Juice" to your DAW. Listen for the arrangement in the stereo mix, and identify the bar where each slice begins. How many macro-samples occur once, and how many repeat?
2. **Rap to the beat.** Import the stereo mix of "PC's Juice" to your DAW. Rap the lyrics of "Juicy" recorded on a separate track.
3. **Rap to the separated files of the beat.** Import the stereo macro- samples and recreate the arrangement of "PC's Juice." Rap the lyrics of "Juicy" recorded on a separate track. Mix to taste.
4. **Create your own beat.** Use the sampler in your DAW to create your own macro-sampled beat and rap that sounds like the east coast renaissance era in hip-hop.

CHAPTER 8

Southern Hip-Hop: MIDI and Music Sequencing

LISTENING: SOUTHERN HIP-HOP

- "Mind Playing Tricks on Me" by the Geto Boys (1991)
- "Make 'Em Say Uhh!" by Master P (1997)
- "What's Your Fantasy" by Ludacris (2000)
- "It's Hard Out Here for a Pimp" by Three 6 Mafia (2005)
- "Lollipop" by Lil Wayne (2008)
- "Super Bass" by Nicki Minaj (2010)

Beat makers in Atlanta, New Orleans, Memphis, Miami, and Houston had been investing in hip-hop soon after they heard "Rapper's Delight" in 1979. But mainstream success just was not available for the southern accent that was being performed on top of the same sort of beat you could hear coming out of New York.

Luther Campbell, PKA Luke Skyywalker, was a Miami-based promoter of rap who booked well-known hip-hop performers for shows in his hometown. He liked the group 2 Live Crew enough that he moved them from California, managed them, and eventually became a group member and lead rapper.

The relocated group released its first album, *The 2 Live Crew Is What We Are*, in 1986 and shocked listeners with highly sexualized lyrics more suited for the strip club than the dance club. Their sound was emulative of Run DMC's work that used sparse drum machine patterns punctuated by distorted guitars. But instead of moving toward a more natural drum sound by using the Linn or Oberheim drum machines that contained samples, the 2 Live Crew opted to maximize the Roland TR-808, the by now cast-off and almost forgotten drum machine based on synthetic tones. "Throw the D" (1986), from *The 2 Live Crew Is What We Are*, is a 124 bpm all-TR-808 drum machine beat with stuttered music and vocal samples from "Dance to the Drummer's Beat" by Herman Kelly & Life (1978), "Al-Naafiysh (the Soul)" by Hashim (1983), "Change the Beat" by Beside (1982), and "Planet Rock" by Afrika Bambaataa and the Soulsonic Force (1982). The hip-hop tradition of record scratching and appropriating samples was a central part of their record making, as the 2 Live Crew broke through to larger and larger audiences with simple beats and pornography-laced lyrics, their sound would eventually come to be known as "Miami bass."

A prominently noticeable feature of the Miami bass sound is the lack of bass lines, real or synthetic, in any of their compositions. The bass guitar and bass synthesizer were simply replaced by the low-frequency energy of the TR-808's kick drum. The low-frequency tone of the TR-808 is a static pitch vibrating at about 100 Hz, and this tone alone is what Luke Skyywalker used on all the 2 Live Crew material. Talk about rebellious and innovative!

In 1997, following the deaths of Tupac and Biggie, southern hip-hop was finally ready to do serious battle with the entrenched hip-hop empires on the east and west coasts.

The southern accent that had been struggling to be heard in previous years moved to the forefront on "Make 'Em Say Uhh!" by Master P (1997), a single heard on the album *Ghetto D*. This composition, moving at 85 bpm, felt different than much of the east coast–influenced southern hip-hop that had come before. It contained the prerequisite TR-808 drum machine sounds, no bass line, a sample from "Apache" by the Sugarhill Gang (1981), and an interpolation of the lyric and melody from "Funkbox Party" by the Masterdon Committee (1982). It also had a sixteenth-note hi-hat pattern that, on first listen, sounded a lot like your average hip-hop record from either coast in 1997. But something was different. The video for this song revealed that the tempo was not 85 bpm, but actually the more frenetic 170 bpm that each of the people in the video seemed to be "bouncing" to. Yes, it is true that you can create this composition at either tempo, but when you watch the video you can feel the quarter-note bounce of the performers at 170 bpm, not an eighth-note bounce at 85 bpm.

This differentiation of sequencing tempo is important because it affects the subdivisions of the music sequencer when you are programming your samples, kick and snare patterns, and even more specifically, your hi-hat patterns. If you don't watch the Master P music video to "Make 'Em Say Uhh!," this could slip by you, and you would hear the same "boom-bap" relationship between the kick and the snare that is a hallmark of both east and west coast hip-hop. Even the hi-hat figure wouldn't sound remarkable. But when the rapper Mystikal enters the 5:11 song at the 3:46 mark, you can really hear the innovation that southern hip-hop infused into hip-hop music.

As southern hip-hop seized on this polyrhythmic device, tempos got slower and slower to accommodate the double-time feel, and then seemed to go around the tempo clockface with a fluidity that went out from an 80 bpm center point. The South had found its unique slant on hip-hop. These slower tempos are a perfectly nuanced variation for the heat-baked lifestyles of rappers from the southern United States.

Cash Money Records and No Limit Records both aided in showcasing New Orleans as a hub of southern hip-hop. Hypnotize Minds, a label out of Memphis, would weigh in with a strong showing due to the Oscar win for Three 6 Mafia's "It's Hard Out Here for a Pimp" (2005). By 2002, southern hip-hop accounted for more than half of the singles on the *Billboard* hip-hop music charts, and that trend continued into 2003, 2004, and 2005. In part because of the late 1990s successes of the production company Organized Noize and the record label So So Def Recordings, Atlanta is now recognized as the center for all things hip-hop.

TEMPO

Southern hip-hop tempos range between 80 bpm and 160 bpm but can be programmed with a polyrhythmic urgency by double-timing the sequencer when the producer wants to get slower than 80 bpm. This may seem like a simple idea, but it was a groundbreaking modification, allowing southern hip-hop its own unique spin on hip-hop.

There was a polyrhythmic *bounce* that allowed for more complex rhyme schemes at this tempo. "Make 'Em Say Uhh!" by Master P (1997) showcased Mystical's extremely fast rhying over an 85 bpm to perfection. By the 2000s the implied bounce available at slower tempos had become a specific performance parameter of hi-hats and stuttered snare drums using the sounds of the TR-808 drum machine. From Ludacris' 140-bpm (read 70 bpm) "What's Your Fantasy" (2000) to Three 6 Mafia's Oscar winning 80 bpm "Hard Out Here for a Pimp" (2005) to Lil Jon's' 82 bpm "Snap Yo Fingers" (2006), southern hip-hop definitely slowed down the grooves of the east and west coasts, but introduced a more complex application of polyrhythms that permeates modern hip-hop to this day.

INSTRUMENTATION

Southern hip-hop's instrumentation has evolved from the early east and west coast setups of an MPC sampler/sequencer and various sound modules. You can still see hardware devices such as the MPC in recording environments, but as the twenty-first century unfolded, more and more southern beat makers began programming their music in software audio and sequencing programs retrofitted with a wide variety of plugins that served as their virtual instruments.

Samples of major drum machine kits—especially 808 kicks, snares, hi-hats, and claps—are must-haves if you are attempting to take on a southern hip-hop composition. Macro-samples are less and less of a must-have in southern hip-hop. It's not that samples are never used; they just became less and less necessary for the body of southern beat making. The bass is usually left to a TR-808 kick drum that can be tuned for melody, or a simple low-frequency sine-tone synthesizer that can drop to notes like C1 (32.7 Hz), B0 (30.8 Hz), or lower.

The ability to tune low frequency kick drums to lower and lower notes creates a bigger sounding composition even though only a few instruments are playing. The 808 kicks have a bit of harmonic content above the fundamental frequency. This allows the 808 to fill the bottom resonance of your composition up to about 200 Hz.

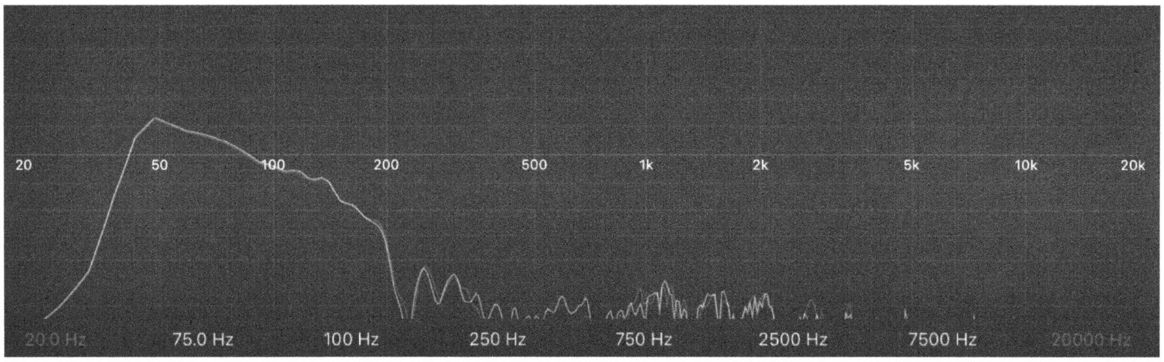

FIG. 8.1. A G1 808 Electronic Kick with Harmonic Energy Around Its 49 Hz Centerpoint

Sine tones have no harmonic content other than the fundamental frequency, so they are preferred when you want a clean low end free of upper harmonics in your beat.

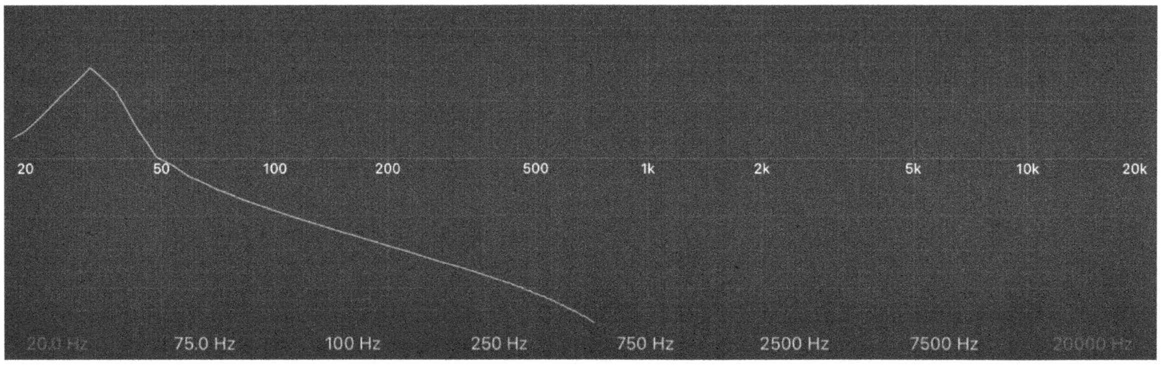

FIG. 8.2. A C1 Sine Tone with No Harmonic Energy Around Its 32.7 Hz Centerpoint

RHYTHMIC FEEL

As in most black American music, there is a call-and-response or tension-and-release aspect to southern hip-hop. It is not emphasized by a variation in instrumentation, but by a variation in rhythmic patterns and/or sonic density. Hi-hat patterns in 1997 were simple eighth-note figures that were performed throughout the composition. Eventually, those upper-frequency patterns would be programmed to enter and exit the compositions, like the triangle figure from "Snap Yo Fingers" by Lil Jon (2006) or the hi-hat figure from "My Chick Bad" by Ludacris (2010). The eighth notes feel like sixteenth notes when counting at 85 bpm, but if you change your metronome to 170 bpm, you can hear the simple eighth note holding court.

Rick Ross' "Hustlin'" (2008) reveals thirty-second notes at a tempo of 136 bpm, along with stuttered claps and stuttered 808 snares. The polyrhythms explored in this period of hip-hop would open a wide range of rhythmic creativity to later southern compositions. The tom-toms and scratches used in east and west coast hip-hop as the push to the downbeat were replaced by implied instrumental rhythms or vocals that delivered the punch for the audience.

SONIC DENSITY

Call and response can be felt in the tension and release of the low frequencies in much of southern hip-hop. The "wait for it" moments when the TR-808 kick is tacit, and then *boom-boom* when it enters, are hallmarks of southern beat making, which have been so successful that pop music has also absorbed the concept. Southern hip-hop has explored a wide range of sonic density, from Master P's orchestra hits in "Make 'Em Say Uhh!" to Nicki Minaj's's EDM-inspired synths in "Super Bass," from drum machine–only compositions all the way up to dense organ and synth compositions like Rick Ross' "Hustlin'" and Lil Wayne's "Lollipop."

Southern hip-hop beat making has evolved over time, but it is primarily driven by sparse, TR-808 drum machine beats in the 80 bpm range that rely on the vocal as the final instrument driving home the character of the composition.

It may sound like a simple realization, but as I was teaching beat making, I was led more and more to teaching my students the essence of rapping in order for the full complexity of sonic characteristics and rhythmic diversity to be understood. The human voice in hip-hop continues to reveal itself as an instrument so powerful that it needs no musical or rhythmic accompaniment to hold the listener's attention. I firmly believe this reality was arrived at incrementally as a byproduct of frequency and rhythmic exploration during the southern hip-hop era.

MIDI AND MUSIC SEQUENCING

Southern hip-hop moves away from a reliance on samples of soul, funk, or disco records. Simple step-sequencing of drum-machine rhythms pulled in audiences without needing the crutch of familiarity that sampling lends to a composition. The music sequencer and a few pieces of MIDI gear are all that were needed to make a southern hip-hop hit. You can hear the sparse synthesizer and drum machine groove on Lil Jon's "Snap Yo Fingers" (2006). Coming in at 82 bpm, this is a classic slice of southern hip-hop. You can also hear that sparseness in Ludacris' evolution from the 140 bpm groove of "What's Your Fantasy" (2001), to the faster 85 bpm groove of "My Chick Bad" (2010). Remember, 85 bpm double-timed is 170 bpm, which is faster than 140 bpm.

"Lollipop" by Lil Wayne (2008) is the perfect example of the sparse instrumentation in a southern hip-hop composition.

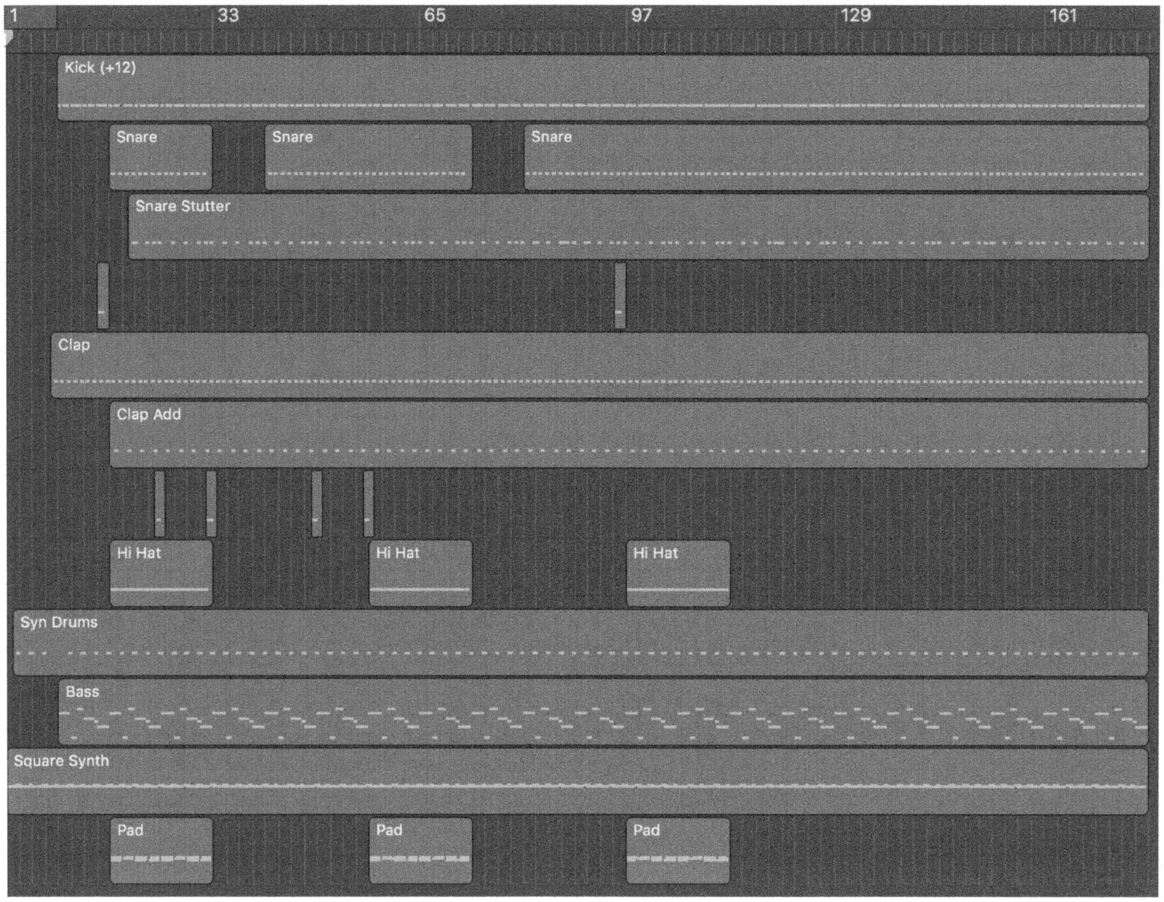

FIG. 8.3. Sequenced MIDI data of "Lollipop" by Lil Wayne (2008)

ACTIVITIES CHAPTER 8

Listening

Using your favorite playback app, listen to "Me So Horny" by the 2 Live Crew (1989), "Mind Playing Tricks on Me" by the Geto Boys (1991), "Make 'Em Say Uhh!" by Master P (1997), "What's Your Fantasy" by Ludacris (2000), "It's Hard Out Here for a Pimp" by Three 6 Mafia (2005), "Lollipop" by Lil Wayne (2008), "Super Bass" by Nicki Minaj (2010). Make note of the tempo, instrumentation, rhythmic feel and sonic density. What are the similarities and differences between these compositions? Can you identify the macro-samples in these compositions? Are there modern compositions that sound like they are influenced by this Southern aesthetic? If so, where are those producers from? When you feel that you have sufficiently analyzed these compositions, move on to the production exercises for this chapter.

Production

Download

DAW Track 8.1 PC's Lollipop

Access the practice files for these activities via the link and code on the first page of this book.

1. **Listen to the beat.** Import the stereo mix of "PC's Lollipop." Listen to the polyrhythmic feel of the composition. Make a list of the instruments that are performing in double time and those that are performing in half time.
2. **Rap to the beat.** Import the stereo mix of "PC's Lollipop. Rap the lyrics of "Lollipop" recorded on a separate track.
3. **Rap to the separated files of the beat.** Import the individual files to have control over each sound. Rap the lyrics of "Lollipop" on a separate track. Mix to taste.
4. **Create your own beat.** Use the virtual instruments in your DAW to create your own beat and rap that sounds like the southern era in hip-hop.

CHAPTER 9

Midwest Hip-Hop: A Regional Hybrid

LISTENING: MIDWEST HIP-HOP

- "Runnin'" by Pharcyde (1995)
- "My Name Is" by Eminem (1999)
- "Hot in Herre" by Nelly (2002)
- "Through the Wire" by Kanye West (2003)
- "Love Lockdown" by Kanye West (2008)

Hybrid regional variation occurs in the music of Midwest beat making. Grooves incorporate east coast, west coast, and southern concepts in tempos that range from 90 to 180 bpm, with an epicenter around 90 bpm. Hip-hop producers like J Dilla (Detroit), No I.D. and Kanye West (Chicago), and Hi-Tek (Cincinnati) each gravitated toward their own stylizations of hip-hop, influenced by the other regional drivers of the art form. Midwest rappers pushed hip-hop lyrical versatility in compositions like the Pharcyde's "Runnin'" (1995), Eminem's "My Name Is" (1999), Nelly's "Hot in Herre" (2002), and Kanye West's imaginative technique of sampling displayed on *The College Dropout* (2004).

Midwest hip-hop began to flower in the mid to late 1980s in cities like Topeka, KS; Milwaukee, WI; and Omaha, NE, before spreading to the urban centers of Chicago, IL; Cleveland, Columbus, Dayton, Cincinnati, and Youngstown, OH; Gary and Hammond, IN; St. Louis, MO; Minneapolis–St. Paul, MN; Louisville, KY; Rochester and Buffalo, NY; Virginia Beach, VA; and any other city with a large population of young black artists that wasn't New York, Los Angeles, or Atlanta.

Beat makers like J Dilla (James Yancey) had been toiling at developing a signature sound since 1992. In 1995, Dilla's group 1st Down became the first hip-hop group from Detroit to sign with a major label. Dilla's sound was raw, unquantized, musically proficient, and sufficiently rebellious. His turntable work—using a Technics MK II, Akai MPC3000, and E-mu SP-1200—(where he sampled himself and others playing instruments) created a musical landscape that still haunts many as a hallmark of creative introspection in hip-hop beat making.

"Runnin'" by the Pharcyde displays a fusion of R&B vocalizing with a raw, unquantized SP-1200 hip-hop beat, a call-and-response bass line playing quarter-note drones on the tonic, and a cool sample of "Saudade Vem Correndo" by Stan Getz (1963, the left side of the mix only) for the main guitar rhythm.

In 1999, the emergence of Eminem (Marshall Mathers) brought a focus to the Midwest as its own hub of creativity, which it had not been prior to his phenomenal success. West coast beat-making legend and record producer Dr. Dre helmed the beat-making and production duties for Eminem's debut recording, *My Name Is* (1999). A sample of "Remember My Song" (1974) by Labi Siffre set up the musical punctuation that was offset by a self-effacing, comical rap performance by Eminem, a superbly talented artist from the Detroit area.

Nelly debuted his album *Country Grammar* in 2000, which shone a spotlight on St. Louis but also on the production team known as the Neptunes, who were based in Virginia Beach. "Hot in Herre," the single from that album, is a beat-driven composition with an interesting chorused electric piano figure playing triads. The simple piano part even includes a chromatic descent, creating a harmonic tension that is simultaneously pop and underground—an achievement that the Neptunes replicated often in their production careers.

Perhaps the best-known of all the Midwest beat makers and artists is Kanye West. Born in Atlanta, claiming Chicago as his hometown, and residing in California, Kanye's personal journey as an artist has been equally matched by his journey as a beat maker. A lover of the TR-808 (he named an album *808s & Heartbreak* in 2008),

Kanye is frequently seen performing with his beat-making tool, the MPC3000. Chillingly creative, innovative, and rebellious, Kanye has introduced his own nuances to the ever-growing palette of hip-hop skills. Specifically, he often used his sampling technique to alter the pitch of an original recording into a "chipmunk" range for the purposes of working it into a composition. Critics and fans fell in love with his out-of-the-ordinary musical thought process explored on "Through the Wire," where Chaka Khan's "Through the Fire" (1984) was pitched up a major third from A♭ major to C major, as a backdrop for his story of overcoming the odds in life. This Midwest brand of beat making was dubbed "chipmunk soul" and would eventually become a technique explored by east, west, and southern beat makers.

Kanye went on to further explore minimalism in a unique way with "Love Lockdown" in 2008. This composition was brought together by combining the low-frequency instruments of the TR-808 drum machine with African percussion instruments (and rhythms) and sparse piano stylings. This musical bed underscored an artistic exploration of his voice as a synthetic instrument by driving it through guitar amplifiers, vocoders, the talkbox, and digital voice synthesizers such as Auto-Tune.

Kanye continually stretches his creative resources and stays true to the underlying hip-hop ideals of innovation and rebelliousness.

TEMPO

Midwest hip-hop tempos range between 90 bpm and 180 bpm. This looks a lot like the circular range of southern hip-hop, but the focus is a bit faster and sits more firmly around 90 bpm, rather than the 80 bpm midpoint of southern hip-hop. The influence of all three regional tempo ranges can actually be felt in Midwest hip-hop compositions.

INSTRUMENTATION

Because of the hybrid regional influences, Midwest hip-hop compositions utilize the full spectrum of hip-hop's creative tools. Turntables, live musicians, drum machines, synthesizers, MIDI programming, music sequencing, sampling, and synthetic vocal processing pop up on the records of artists representing the heartland of America.

RHYTHMIC FEEL

There is an eighth-note urgency similar to that of east and west coast compositions that permeates much of the early music of Midwest beat makers and producers. As the twenty-first century unfolded and southern hip-hop increased in popularity, thirty-second-note figures began to appear more commonly in the compositions.

J Dilla stands out among Midwest hip-hop producers for a production sound that is rhythmically quantized yet "sloppy' at the same time. "Runnin'" by Pharcyde (1995) has snares and kicks within each bar that are intentionally unquantized.

However, the first kick of each bar is in a quantized position. This overlapping of quantized and unquantized elements was a Dilla trademark that merged the drum machine and the skills of a drummer into infectious beat making.

Notice that the snares at bar 6/2/000 and bar 6/4/000 are behind the beat.

A one-bar unquantized drum programming sequence.

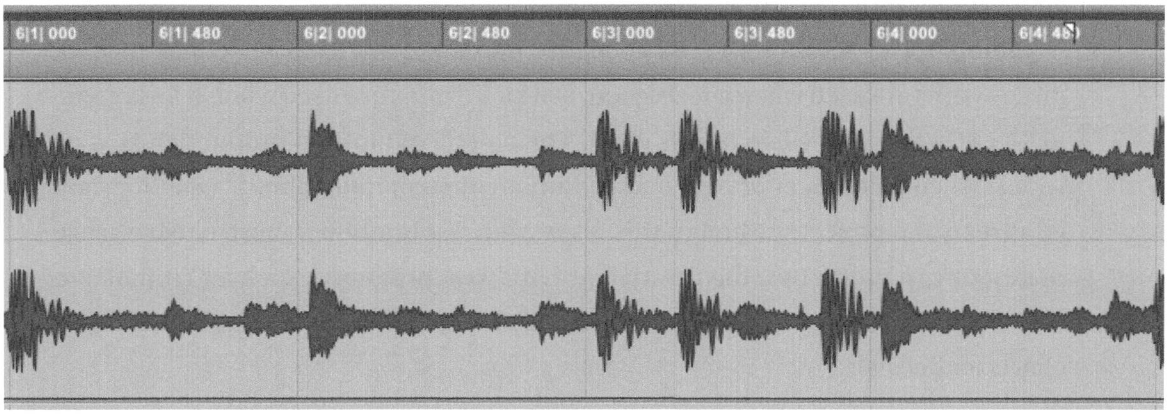

The 6/2/000 snare is 29 ms late.

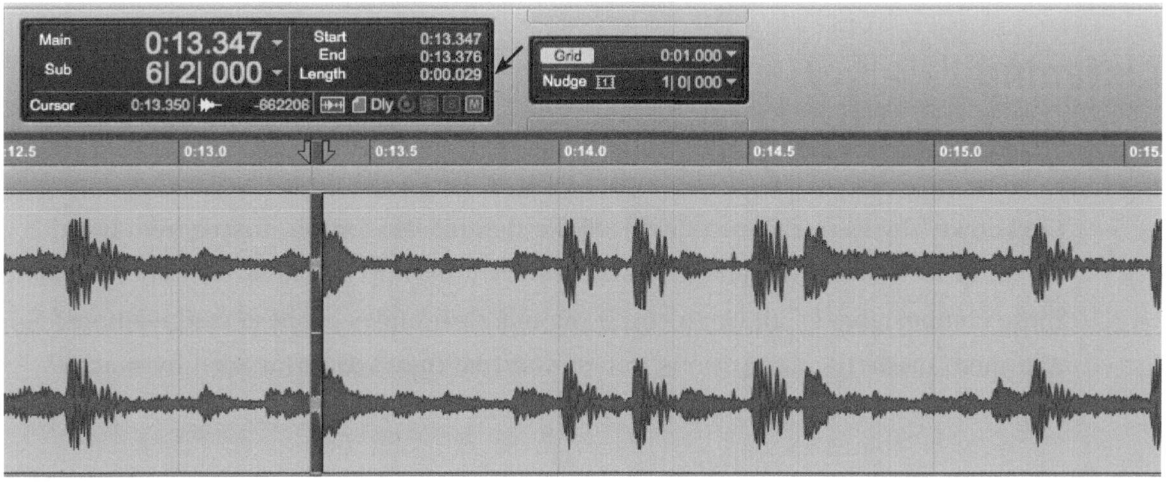

The 6/4/000 snare is 30 ms late.

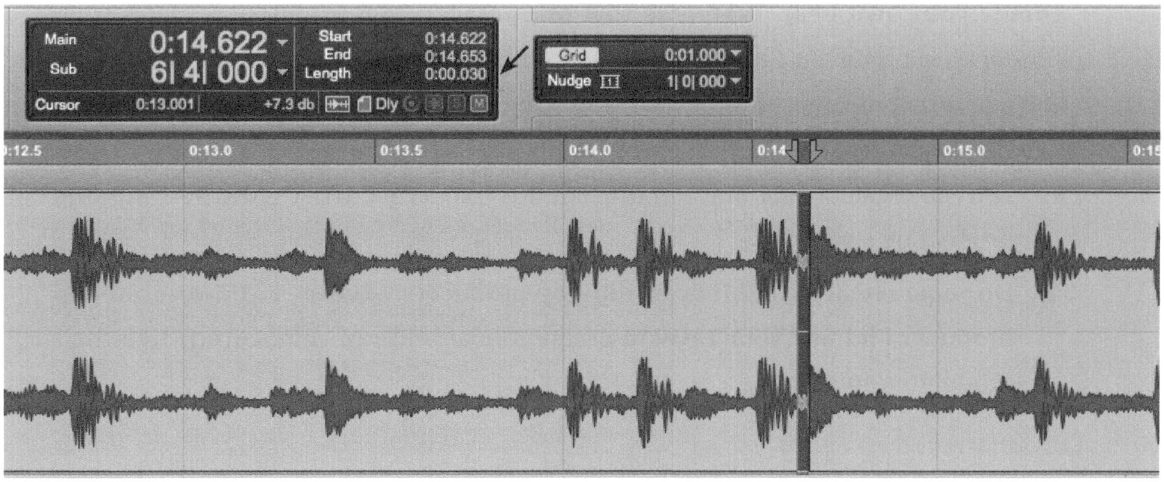

FIG. 9.1. J Dilla Style Quantization

SONIC DENSITY

The sonic density of Midwest hip-hop covers the gamut of the three main regional genres: east coast, west coast, and southern. From the highly exploratory east coast–influenced beats of J Dilla, to the equally exploratory, future-leaning compositions of Kanye West, Midwest hip-hop beat makers and producers have allegiance only to connectivity with their audiences.

Sampling is used when it feels good, live musicians are used when it feels good, disco synths are used when it feels good, 808 kick drums are used when it feels good, EDM LFOs are used when it feels good. The palette of hip-hop production is at its widest when a producer or beat maker with an open opinion about "what hip-hop is" directs the project. Although this gives Midwest hip-hop a more elusive sense of descriptive properties, the creativity of Midwest producers such as Timbaland, the Neptunes, and Kanye West has been peppering the top of the hip-hop and pop charts for decades.

ACTIVITIES CHAPTER 9

Listening

Listen to "Runnin'" by Pharcyde (1995), "My Name Is" by Eminem (1999), "Hot in Herre" by Nelly (2002), "Through the Wire" by Kanye West (2003), and "Love Lockdown" by Kanye West (2008)). Make note of the tempo, instrumentation, rhythmic feel, and sonic density. What are the similarities and differences between these compositions? Can you identify the macro-samples in these compositions? Are there modern compositions that sound like they are influenced by macro-sampling? If so, where are those producers from?

Production

Create your own beat. Take note that Midwest hip-hop production varies from producer to producer. Live, sequencing, and sampling techniques are used in an eclectic mix of influences from the three other dominant hip-hop regions.

1. Choose an artist from the listening exercises. Use the virtual instruments in your DAW to create a beat and rap that sounds like a that artist's Midwest hip-hop production style.
2. Do some research on Midwest hip-hop producers. Choose a Midwest hip-hop producer and use your DAW to create a beat and rap that sounds like their production style.

PART III

Hip-Hop's Expanded Reach

The success and proliferation of hip-hop has given the world a wide range of music making that lives under the umbrella of hip-hop. Regional variations have given way to subgenres within regions. The popular music industry uses hip-hop to reach its ever-evolving youthful demographic. Beat makers throughout the globe have absorbed the skill set of creativity embraced by hip-hop. Rappers and singers are exploring different sonic horizons for their voices. Outlined in this section are features of subgenres resulting from the expanded reach of hip-hop's global acceptance.

CHAPTER 10

Hip-Hop Subgenres

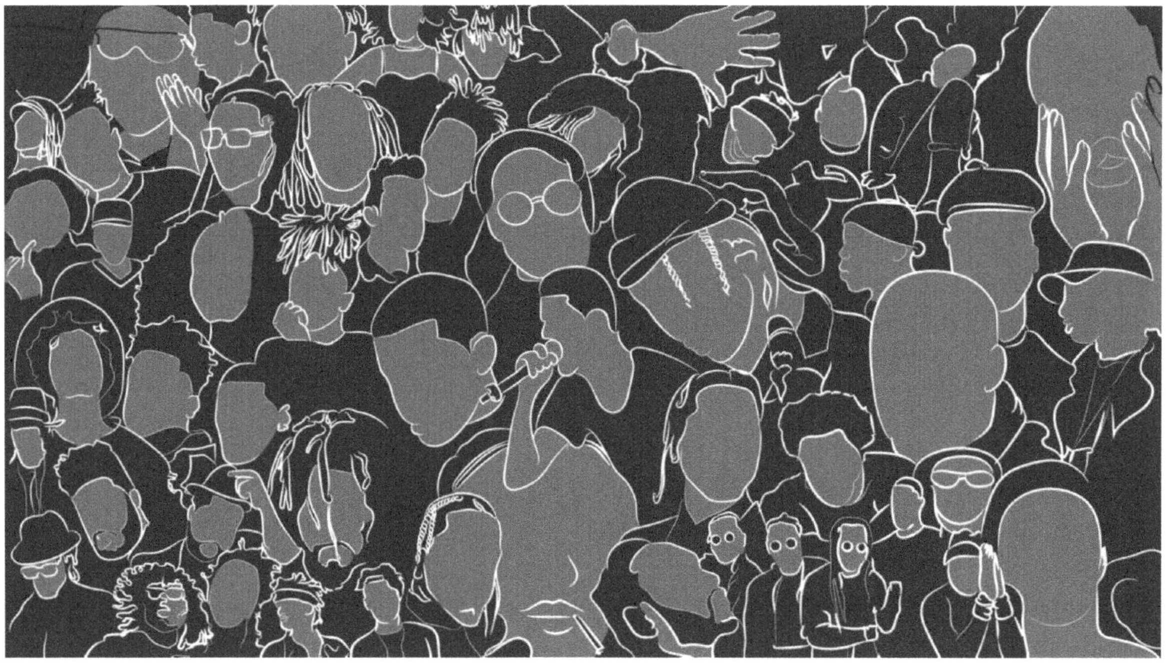

Before "Rapper's Delight," all hip-hop music was underground. In the modern era, underground hip-hop is usually associated with independent artists who distribute their own music or who might have some sort of deal with an independent label that provides the artist with an elevated level of promotion, marketing, and distribution. Some of these artists and producers are underground because they are committed to being anti-commercial; some are underground because of political stances that are not popular for "mainstream" consumption; and some are underground because they haven't yet figured out how to be commercial, but they are trying every day.

Hip-hop itself was an underground phenomenon that found its way to commercial viability, even as it continued to struggle with social acceptability. But, in many ways, that is what rebellious and innovative music will always be—a bit socially awkward, uncomfortable, and unacceptable.

Although the following is not a list of all the subgenres of hip-hop, it does represent a few of the important developments within our discussed regions.

SUBGENRES ORIGINATING ON THE EAST COAST

Boom Bap

LISTENING: BOOM BAP

- "Eric B. Is President" by Eric B. and Rakim (1986)
- "They Reminisce Over You (T.R.O.Y.)" by Pete Rock and CL Smooth (1992)
- "The Most Beautifullest Thing in This World" by Keith Murray (1994)
- "NY State of Mind" by Nas (1994)

When drum machines made their debut in 1980, hip-hop producers programmed them like the break beats in records. The drum machine added texture and additional rhythmic possibilities to beat playback coming from, or inspired by, turntable looping.

When cost-effective samplers emerged in 1987, a beat maker was able to retain the sound of a record via sampling while imposing the flexibility of a drum machine's progamability on the beat making process.

"Boom bap" is the sound your drums make if you are an east coast hip-hop producer with an ear for extracting breakbeat samples from 1960s soul and 1970s funk music. "Boom" is the sound the kick drum makes, and "bap" is the sound the snare makes in an old school east coast hip-hop sampled beat like those found on the album *Return of the Boom Bap* by Krs-One (1993). The result of this sampling technique is a fluid drum performance with a pre-recorded sheen that focuses on a heavy kick, snare, and hi-hat performance in a cyclical loop.

Even now, the underlying boom bap drum signature remains a staple of east coast beat making, showing up in the music of east coast icons Jay-Z and Nas.

Conscious

Listening: Conscious

- "The Message" by Grandmaster Flash and the Furious Five ft. Melle Mel (1982)
- "Dear Mama" by 2Pac (1995)
- "White America" by Eminem (2002)
- "Glory" by John Legend and Common (2015)

Conscious hip-hop is primarily differentiated from other forms of hip-hop by its lyrical content. Although you can currently hear conscious hip-hop across the regional spectrum, the seeds were planted on the east coast.

Political, cultural, philosophical, economic, and social themes can all fall under the scope of the rapper's word play; the beat maker provides the backdrop for that content.

Even deeper within conscious hip-hop are themes of Afro-centricity, religion, the rejection of crime and violence, and the struggles of common peoples' lives. Although most of Public Enemy's and N.W.A's music can be considered conscious in its anti-dominant culture stance, a song like "Dear Mama" by 2Pac informs us of our common humanity through a man's love for his mother, and her life's struggles.

Conscious hip-hop was lauded by the mainstream on February 22, 2015, when "Glory" by John Legend and Common won the Oscar for Best Original Song.

Mafioso

Listening: Mafioso

- "Fast Life" by Kool G Rap (1995)
- "Can't Knock the Hustle" by Jay-Z (1996)
- "Ten Crack Commandments" by the Notorious B.I.G. (1997)
- "Mafia Music" by Rick Ross (2009)

Mafioso rap is the east coast equivalent of west coast's gangsta rap. The lyrical themes reference the lavish lifestyles and behavior of organized crime. Credit for Mafioso rap goes to Kool G Rap, with his album and title cut "Road to the Riches" (1989).

More life was given to this east coast hardcore movement in 1995, when *Only Built 4 Cuban Linx* by Raekwon, *Doe or Die* by AZ, and *4,5,6* by Kool G Rap were all released. Mainstream recognition having been attained, these albums opened the door for other works like *Reasonable Doubt* by Jay-Z, *Life After Death* by the

Notorious B.I.G., and *It Was Written* by Nas.

The 2000s saw yet another resurgence of Mafioso rap with *Fishscale* by Ghostface Killah, *American Gangster* by Jay-Z, and *La Bella Mafia* by Lil' Kim. Even more recently, artists such as Rick Ross, T.I., Fabolous, Jadakiss, Jim Jones, and Cassidy have created entries into this gritty subgenre.

Mafioso tells full stories and is, by nature, an album-driven genre.

SUBGENRES ORIGINATING ON THE WEST COAST

Chicano (Los Angeles) and Latino (Miami, New York)

LISTENING: CHICANO AND LATINO

- "La Raza" by Kid Frost (1990)
- "Insane in the Brain" by Cypress Hill (1993)
- "How We Roll" by Big Pun (2001)
- "Make It Rain" by Fat Joe (2007)
- "Timber" by Pitbull (2014)

Although there has been a Latino presence throughout hip-hop from the beginning, Mellow Man Ace (a Cuban American) is credited as the Godfather of Latin Rap with the first bilingual hit for a Latino hip-hop artist, "Mentirosa" (1989). Kid Frost debuted in 1990 with his album *Hispanic Causing Panic*. Frost's hit single "La Raza" (1990) signaled the rise of Chicano hip-hop's commercial presence—a presence that spoke to a southwest and Midwest Mexican-American lifestyle, mirroring the successes of gangsta rap. The early 1990s proved a boon period for Chicano hip-hop. This period saw successful singles released by A.L.T., the Latin Alliance (a collaboration between Kid Frost, Mellow Man Ace, A.L.T., and other Chicano rappers), A Lighter Shade of Brown, Cypress Hill, and Brownside.

The first Latino group with platinum sales (one million units) was Cypress Hill, who hailed from South Gate, California, seven miles southeast of downtown Los Angeles. Big Pun, a rapper of Puerto Rican descent from the Bronx, NY, is the first Latino solo artist with platinum sales of a rap album. Mexican culture is fêted in Chicano hip-hop, and Latino culture is also embraced through the work of New York artists such as Fat Joe, the Beatnuts, Chino XL, the Mesanjarz of Funk, DJ Frankie Cutlass, Cuban Link, Immortal Technique, who speak from a Puerto Rican perspective. Miami artists such as Don Dinero, A.B. Junior, Pitbull, and Qba Libre speak from a Cuban perspective. Multilingualism and Mexican, Puerto Rican, and Cuban versions of Spanglish are running themes in the music of Latino hip-hop. From its earliest roots in Mexican gangsta rap to the chart-topping pop successes of Pitbull, Latino rap continues to make its presence felt domestically and internationally.

Hyphy (Oakland)

LISTENING: HYPHY

- "Tell Me When to Go" by E-40 (2006)
- "Thizzle Dance" by Mac Dre (2002)
- "Super Hyphy" by Keak Da Sneak (2005)
- "Blow the Whistle" by Too Short (2006)

The west coast in general, and the Bay Area specifically, feel that their version of the origins of hip-hop has been excluded by the more accepted narrative that hip-hop began in the Bronx circa 1973. This exclusion is due in part to New York's dominance of the music industry at that time and a muting of cultural expression by local authorities following the release of the spoken word album *Rappin' Black in a White World* by The Watts Prophets (1971). Even though it may have been muted, west coast hip-hop culture produced DJs, rappers , dancers, and graffiti artists contemporary to their east coast counterparts throughout the 1970s and 1980s, albeit without the same acclaim or celebrity until NWA in 1987.

By the 1990s, in Oakland specifically, the hyperactive hip-hop culture of California's Bay Area was coined "hyphy" by Keak Da Sneak on an EP titled *The Autopsy* (1994). The synth led, staccato beat making reflects west coast culture, language, graffiti, and dances like "going dumb" and "ghostriding the whip." Hyphy culture has had a continuous evolution since the mid-1990s, and has seen a resurgence due to the work of DJ Mustard, a Los Angeles–based DJ who is taking inspiration from his Northern California neighbors.

Ratchet (Los Angeles)

LISTENING: RATCHET

- "Rack City" by Tyga (2011)
- "Show Me" by Kid Ink ft. Chris Brown (2013)
- "I Don't F*** With You" by Big Sean ft. E-40 (2014)
- "Be Real" by Kid Ink ft. DeJ Loaf (2015)
- "Needed Me" by Rihanna (2016)

The main protagonist of ratchet music, DJ Mustard, is a Los Angeles–based DJ and record producer who draws his inspiration from the Northern California hyphy movement. Ratchet tracks groove from synthesizer lines more than from drums. In fact, the drums usually disappear for extended periods of time in ratchet tracks.

A quarter- or eighth-note synthesizer pulse is used as the glue that holds the track together instead of the standard drum and percussion sounds.

SUBGENRES ORIGINATING IN THE SOUTH

Crunk (Memphis)

LISTENING: CRUNK

- "Get Low" by Lil Jon & the East Side Boyz ft. the Ying Yang Twins (2003)
- "Yeah!" by Usher ft. Lil Jon and Ludacris (2004)
- "Goodies" by Ciara ft. Petey Pablo (2004)
- "Freek-A-Leek" by Petey Pablo (2004)
- "Run It!" By Chris Brown ft. Juelz Santana (2005)

Crunk is a hip-hop subgenre that began in the dance and club scenes of Memphis, Tennessee in the early 1990s. It is an upbeat sound based on repetitive synthesizer and bass with drums serving as tension and release. The word "crunk" is a past-tense variation of "to crank up," and similar to hyphy in Northern California, is connected to its own dances and overall "crunk" attitude and lifestyle. Beat makers in the crunk tradition stay away from sampling, probably to avoid costly sampling clearance negotiations.

Snap (Atlanta)

LISTENING: SNAP

- "Laffy Taffy" by D4L (2005)
- "Wait (The Whisper Song)" by the Ying Yang Twins (2005)
- "Snap Yo Fingers" by Lil Jon ft. E-40 and Sean P (2006)
- "Crank That (Soulja Boy)" by Soulja Boy (2007)
- "Buy U A Drank (Shawty Snappin')" by T-Pain (2007)

Snap is derived from crunk in a way similar to ratchet being derived from hyphy. The crunk sound of early 1990s Memphis was taken by beat makers in Atlanta and turned into a new sound called snap. A main variation is the use of a finger snapping sound for the backbeat instead of claps or snares. Group vocal sounds and whistling are also used effectively in snap. Sampling in hip-hop by the early to mid-2000s had become the creative tool of artists with large budgets who were flaunting their ability to pay costly sample clearance costs, so snap beat makers, like most southern beat makers, preferred music sequencing to record sampling.

Bounce (New Orleans)

LISTENING: BOUNCE

- "Where They At" by DJ Jimi (1992)
- "Pump Tha Party" by Partners-N-Crime (1995)
- "Back That Azz Up" by Juvenile ft. Mannie Fresh and Lil Wayne (1999)
- "Wobble Baby" by V.I.C. (2008)
- "Gin in My System" by Big Freedia (2010)

It only makes sense that New Orleans, Louisiana would weigh in with its own take on the upbeat sound of hip-hop. Bounce is sparse music infused with New Orleans–style percussion, Mardi Gras–like chanting, the driving sound of the 808 drum machine, some turntable scratching, and in more recent versions, live or synthesized brass sounds. Most bounce beat makers stay away from sampling except where a vocal sample might be used to emphasize lyrics in the track. Bounce continues to thrive even though its origins date back to the late 1980s. Spearheaded by artists like Big Freedia, the "sissy bounce" movement is an evolution of New Orleans bounce culture that has found a worldwide audience and reality television success for Freedia herself. Bounce, like crunk, hyphy, and chopped and screwed (Houston, Texas), is a highly localized regional variation of the main hip-hop regional styles.

Trap (Atlanta)

LISTENING: TRAP

- "Hard in Da Paint" by Waka Flocka Flame (2010)
- "Blowin' Money Fast" by Rick Ross ft. Styles P (2010)
- "Turn on the Lights" by Future (2012)
- "Panda" by Desiigner (2015)
- "Trap Queen" by Fetty Wap (2015)

Primarily fueled by lyrics that glorify urban street life, trap beats are in line with southern beat-making tradition in that no samples are used. The 808 drum sounds are a staple, with hi-hats that are double- and triple-timed. The 808 snare serves double duty as a backbeat instrument and as a double- and triple-timed percussive fill instrument. There are variants of trap, such as drill in Chicago, represented across America and the world. Trap enjoyed a run as a strong subgenre of southern hip-hop from the mid 1990s through the 2000s, but began a run of cultural dominance with the success of "Hard in Da Paint" by Waka Flocka Flame (2010), which was produced by Lex Luger when he was only nineteen years old. Although hip-hop has a broad spectrum of beat making approaches, current emerging hip-hop beat makers' first experimentations with the craft will typically begin with a trap beat, more so than manipulating recorded samples.

The main DAW of trap beat makers is the latest incarnation of Fruity Loops, called FL Studio. FL Studio has created a revolution in southern beat making that rivals the MPC's dominance of the 1990s and 2000s. The pattern-based DAW architecture provides an even a lower barrier of entry for anyone who wants to create sequencer-based music. (Soulja Boy was just seventeen years old when he used a demo version to create his snap anthem "Crank That," in 2010.) Mike WiLL Made-It has succeeded in bringing trap to mainstream audiences with compositions such as "23" ft. Miley Cyrus, Wiz Khalifa, and Juicy J (2013), and urban teens all across America are now listening to trap and its offshoots because urban, rhythmic, and pop radio have all embraced the subgenre.

SUBGENRES ORIGINATING IN THE MIDWEST

Drill (Chicago)

LISTENING: DRILL

- "I Don't Like" by Chief Keef ft. Lil Reese (2012)
- "Chiraq (Remix)" by Montana of 300 (2014)
- "52 Bars" by Lil Durk (2014)
- "Bang Like Chop" by Young Chop (2014)
- "Everyday in Chicago" by G Herbo (2014)

Drill music is very similar to trap music in terms of tempo, instrumentation, rhythmic feel, and song density. Both use lyrical content focusing on weed, violence, guns, and a misogynistic lifestyle. One of the main artistic differences is the regional accent used in the delivery of the lyrical content.

ACTIVITIES CHAPTER 10

Production

Create your own beat. Now is the opportunity to focus on your preferred sub-genre and its stylistic elements. Use this production exercise to become even better at beat making.

1. Choose an artist from the listening exercises. Use the virtual instruments in your DAW to create a beat and rap that sounds like the hip-hop production style of that sub-genre
2. Choose a sub-genre. Do some more research on the producers of that sub-genre. Use your DAW to create a beat and rap that sounds like their production style.

CHAPTER 11

Pop Hip-Hop: 1985 to Present

Listening: Pop Hip-Hop

- "Parents Just Don't Understand" (1989) by Will Smith
- "Gettin' Jiggy Wit It" by Will Smith (1998)
- "Lose Yourself" by Eminem (2002)
- "Run It!" by Chris Brown (2005)
- "Imma Be" by Black Eyed Peas (2009)
- "23" by Mike WiLL Made-It ft. Miley Cyrus, Wiz Khalifa, and Juicy J (2013)
- "Fancy" by Iggy Azalea (2014)
- "My House" by Flo Rida (2016)
- "Bodak Yellow" by Cardi B (2017)
- "I Like It" by Cardi B (2018)
- "Old Town Road" by Lil Nas X (2019)
- "Truth Hurts" by Lizzo (2019)

Hip-hop has had its fair share of popular successes since the undeniable crossover success of "Walk This Way" (1985), but as of July 2017, it was acknowledged by *Billboard*, *Forbes*, and other financial publications as the dominant genre in the United States. Technically, the varying styles and tempos of pop hip-hop draw from any and all resources, but a melodically sung hook in the choruses is a common feature for the large majority of pop-hip-hop songs.

As a marriage of hip-hop beats, raps, melodically sung choruses and wide audience accessibility, pop hip-hop opened the door for the huge success of hip-hop as a genre.

"Parents Just Don't Understand" (1989) by Will Smith won the first Grammy award for Best Hip-Hop Performance in 1989 and is a good example of pop hip-hop formula.

For pop audiences, the incredible oratory skills of white rapper Eminem broke down the color line of rapping as an exclusively African American art form. Although his rise fueled cries of an appropriation of the hip-hop art form, Eminem's verbal skill set was so superior that it solidified his place as a true master worthy of respect from his peers. His success, akin to Elvis's success in early black-dominated rock 'n' roll, opened hip-hop to the ears of even more subsets of the American consumer population.

Pop hip-hop seems to be the natural evolution of the huge connection the genre has with its changing audiences. But pop hip-hop is constantly derided as a sellout form of "pure" hip-hop. Artists who make money through hip-hop, as a pop vehicle, are sometimes seen as compromising the social and political roots of the art form. Every hip-hop beat maker who seeks to cross over from producing in their bedroom to producing for millions of fans puts their artists on the front line of criticism from those who love hip-hop as a vital underground representation of common life.

Newer versions of pop hip-hop, such as "23" (2013, a trap pop record) by Mike WiLL Made-It (ft. Miley Cyrus), Wiz Khalifa, and Juicy J, and Iggy Azalea's "Fancy" (2014, a ratchet pop record) produced by the Invisible Men and the Arcade, were controversial moments of hip-hop success that continue to extend the lexicon of hip-hop music production. Cultural appropriation is an issue with these compositions because white artists were seizing a much larger share of wealth from an art form that black artists have poured blood, sweat, and tears into for decades. "Fancy" sat directly in the path of this scorn because, as a blonde, white, upper-middle-class female from Australia, Iggy Azalea seemed to be the antithesis of what hip-hop stood for at its birth.

Even though cultural messages have become diluted with the extreme popularity of pop hip-hop, it has opened the door for an explosion of talent and diversity that reflects rebellion, innovation, and the quick pace of the twenty-first century's digital age.

In July 2017, hip-hop had officially become the number one selling genre of music in America. In that year, Cardi B became the first solo female rapper to reach number one on the Billboard Hot 100 with her composition "Bodak Yellow (Money

Moves)," a feat that was last achieved with "Doo-Wop (That Thing)" by Lauren Hill (1998).

"Bodak Yellow (Money Moves)" is punctuated with hard hitting 808's from the 808 Warfare sample pack, along with vocal interpolations from "Da' Dip" by Freak Nasty (1996) and "No Flockin" by Kodak Black (2015). Cardi B's production sound continued to be galvanized on another successful number one, "I Like It (2018)," which was replaced by yet another successful number one, "Girls Like You" by Maroon 5 (ft. Cardi B, 2018). This last string of number one Billboard Hot 100 compositions highlighted Cardi B as the first female rapper to replace herself at number one on that chart.

"I Like It" by Cardi B showcases macro-sampling with its use of "I Like It Like That" by Pete Rodriguez (1967) as the main body of the song that is variously sampled and high pass filtered throughout the composition. All of Carli B's work highlights 808 drum machine samples, which is typical of hip-hop artists.

"Old Town Road" by Lil Nas X (2019) became the longest running Billboard Hot 100 song in the chart's history. It highlights the 808 Warfare sample pack once again, and various two-bar sample slices from "34 Ghosts IV" by Nine Inch Nails (2008).

Another composition, "Truth Hurts" by Lizzo (2019), became the longest running number one single from a female rap artist. It features a broad beat making sensibility that reflects Lizzo's Midwest upbringing and those of her New York and Los Angeles writing team.

Pop hip-hop's acceptability by listeners and a shift in the consumption of music to streaming platforms are huge contributing factors toward the success of hip-hop during this post-2015 period of the genre.

ACTIVITIES CHAPTER 11

Listening

Using your favorite playback app, listen to "Bodak Yellow" by Cardi B. Count the number of measures where there is no kick drum. Count the number of measures where there is no bass instrument. Other than the vocal, what is the instrument that never stops? What are the similarities and differences between the compositions on our listening list? When you feel that you have sufficiently analyzed these compositions, move on to the audio exercises for this chapter.

Production

Download

DAW Track 11.1 PC's Yellow

Access the practice files for these activities via the link and code on the first page of this book.

1. **Listen to the beat.** Import the stereo mix of "PC's Yellow" to your DAW. Identify the synthesizer timbres. Make your own chart of where the complex polyrhythmic kick drum pattern enters and exits the composition.
2. **Rap to the beat.** Import the stereo mix of "PC's Yellow" to your DAW. Rap the lyrics of "Bodak Yellow" recorded on a separate track.
3. **Rap to the separated files of the beat.** Import the individual files to have control over each sound. Rap the lyrics of "Bodak Yellow" on a separate track. Mix to taste.
4. **Create your own beat.** Use the virtual instruments in your DAW to create your own beat and rap that reflect the production elements of current pop hip-hop.

CHAPTER 12

Global Hip-Hop

Listening: Global Hip-Hop

- "Pânico Na Zona Sul" by Racionais MC's (1988) from Brazil
- "L'École du Micro d'Argent" by IAM (1997) from France
- "Boomerang" by Daara J (2003) from Senegal
- "Hep Ayni" by Fuat Ergin (2009) from Germany/Turkey
- "100 Bars" by Klash (2017) from Saudi Arabia
- "It G Ma" by Keith Ape (2015) from South Korea
- "Jungli Sher" by Divine (2016) from India
- "One Dance" by Drake (2016) from Canada
- "Despacito" by Luis Fonsi ft. Daddy Yankee (2017) from Puerto Rico

Hip-hop is a global phenomenon, but most listeners of hip-hop have only scratched the surface of the hundreds of countries that have a local version of the art form.

France is the second-largest hip-hop market in the world, and like all of the countries under the global arc of the genre, hip-hop began as an import from America. Soon, there were crude local interpolations and emulations, which over time birthed full-fledged production teams speaking to local audiences, in their languages, about their issues.

The techniques are the same as those in the U.S., but the purpose has usually remained social and political commentary in most of the countries that have imported hip-hop into their culture. While commercial hip-hop in the United States seems to have devolved into a misogynistic, profanity-laced shell of its former self, global hip-hop continues to speak about issues "of the people, by the people, and for the people."

Global hip-hop is represented in Africa, Asia, Europe, the Middle East, North America, Oceania, and South America. The most prevalent beat-making techniques are sampling and music sequencing/MIDI, with turntablism and live band production in the small minority.

EUROPE

Under the heading of European hip-hop charts are the countries in Northern Europe, which include Denmark, Finland, Iceland, Ireland, Norway, Sweden, the United Kingdom, and of the Baltic States. Of note is the grime scene in the U.K., with its rapid-fire rhymes and beats clocking in at 130 to 140 bpm. Grime has never grabbed a foothold in America, but it uses double- and triple-timed wordplay emulative of Midwest artist Twista and southern artist Mystikal.

Central Europe developed its hip-hop movement through the Czech Republic, Hungary, Poland, Slovakia, and Slovenia. Eastern Europe's countries representing a hip-hop aesthetic are Bulgaria, Romania, Russia, and Ukraine. Southern Europe has developed a hip-hop sound in Albania, Kosovo, Bosnia and Herzegovina, Greece, Cyprus, Italy, the Republic of Macedonia, Portugal, Serbia, and Spain.

Western Europe has provided the world with hip-hop from Austria, Belgium, Germany, the Netherlands, Switzerland, and the second-largest hip-hop market in the world, France.

In France, MC Solaar emerged in 1991 as the first iteration of French rap stars. His album *Qui Sème le Vent Récolte le Tempo* led the way for French-language artists such as Dee Nasty and Lionel D to define life as a young French citizen. French hip-hop quickly evolved into more aggressive expression by groups from Paris such as Assassin and Suprême NTM.

Groups from Paris and Marseilles created a rivalry similar to that of New York and Los Angeles, with Paris representing an urban sound and Marseilles representing a more laid-back—although potently aggressive—take on hip-hop.

In 1997, the Marseille group IAM released "L'École du Micro d'Argent," which sold more than one million units and expanded the commercial viability of French hip-hop. Even though the French hip-hop scene has never been wholly supported by the French music industry, it has continued to grow and mirror the emerging innovations of American hip-hop. Social and political themes eventually gave way to gangsta themes, that eventually gave way to Mafioso themes, that eventually gave way to trap and ratchet beat making.

Europe, as a whole, does not have one specific hip-hop sound, but most practitioners have been adept at sampling. Since the 1990s, beat makers have used the MPC music sequencer/sampler. The newest generations of European beat makers are decidedly DAW-based creators, using tools that make beat and pitch analysis fairly easy. Current beat makers, from all countries, use Internet tutorials to match the sonic signatures of American hip-hop to great success.

AFRICA

Hip-hop entered Africa through Senegal, which sits at the westernmost tip of the continent. The first French hip-hop star, MC Solaar, is Senegalese, as is American hip-hop icon Akon, who had several top tens from 2004 through 2008.

After hip-hop arrived on the African continent in the early 1990s, other countries followed suit and embraced it as a social and political voice, including Algeria, Angola, Botswana, Cameroon, Côte d'Ivoire, Democratic Republic of Congo, Gambia, Ghana, Guinea, Kenya, Madagascar, Malawi, Morocco, Namibia, Niger, Nigeria, Rwanda, Sierra Leone, Somalia, South Africa, Tanzania, Togo, Uganda, Zambia, and Zimbabwe.

The hip-hop of Senegal, like that of most of the African countries listed, has such a rich rhythmical tradition to draw on for beat making that a natural fusion of drum machine, music sequencing, and live percussion is almost always present. Even when the percussion elements are not live, macro-samples are used to pull in loops of rhythms from the beat maker's local aesthetic.

Call and response is a natural part of many African countries' discourse due to the heavy influence of *griots*, whose purpose is to verbally recount and remember African history and lineage. Much like preachers in African American churches or the MCs in "Rapper's Delight," the call from the griot, the preacher, and the MC to the audience, and then the audience's response, fuels the connectivity of the group participating in the respective cultures.

Senegalese praise songs bear a striking resemblance to the praise and worship songs practiced by African American church goers, with live bands delivering cutting-edge musical backing tracks to the themes communicated by the choirs. Chance the Rapper is the latest American rapper to explore the use of gospel choirs in his music, having taken the lead from Kanye West before him. That connection is mirrored by Senegalese artists such as Khar Mbaye Madiaga, who is a *gewel* (the Wolof language word for "griot").

Even though there are many languages and dialects present in Senegalese culture, the languages explored in Senegalese hip-hop are the official language, French, and the most common language, Wolof. Dakar, the capital city of Senegal, is the New York or Los Angeles of African hip-hop and serves as one of the main distribution centers of hip-hop culture throughout Africa.

MIDDLE EAST

The Middle Eastern countries of Egypt, Iran, Israel, Kurdistan, Lebanon, Palestine, Saudi Arabia, and Yemen all have young artists that are exploring hip-hop as cultural expression.

Arabic hip-hop has a strong hold on young people in Arab-speaking countries. Strongly rooted in themes of social consciousness and political awareness, Arabic hip-hop is performed in Arabic, local Arabic dialects, English, French, and Berber languages.

The Arab diaspora includes immigrants in North and South America, Europe, West Africa, South and Southeast Asia, and the Caribbean, who share messages of cultural identity through hip-hop music.

Hip-hop music made by Turks in Germany is a huge commercial voice for hip-hop of the Arab speaking world and co-exists alongside the country's thriving "Eurocentric" hip-hop culture. Both hip-hop incarnations represent life in Germany, albeit from two different points of view.

Arabic beat making tools continue to evolve in lockstep with the beat making tools found in American hip-hop, and have had live band, drum machine, music sequencing, sampling, and regional iterations.

ASIA

Asian hip-hop encompasses hip-hop styles from many countries and in many languages. Regions under the umbrella of East Asia include China, Japan, and Korea. Korean hip-hop (K-hip-hop) has dominated the conversation due to the success of Korean pop music (K-pop) and great brand marketing of Korean music in general. The K-pop composition "Gangnam Style" by Berklee's very own Psy (2012) was the first YouTube video to hit one billion views. You can clearly hear the hip-hop-influenced 808 kicks, claps, snares, and vocal chants running through much of the K-pop sound.

Southeast Asian countries Myanmar, the Philippines, Malaysia, Indonesia, and Singapore also have young beat makers and rappers who are experimenting with hip-hop. The efforts to merge indigenous culture and hip-hop continue to be works in progress that are still developing beat making signatures unique to each country.

The South Asian countries of India, Bangladesh, Nepal, and Pakistan have had huge success with Desi (South Asian diaspora) hip-hop. In particular, the marriage of hip-hop with the successful Indian Bollywood film industry has helped the proliferation of hip-hop across South Asian countries. Rappers like Snoop Dogg have appeared in films (*Singh Is Kinng*, 2008) that have united traditional Indian percussion grooves with the rhythms of hip-hop.

NORTH AMERICA

Beyond the United States, the reggaeton sound that originated in Puerto Rico circa the late 1990s is being mined by hip-hop artists for its danceability. Reggaeton is an important variation of hip-hop that incorporates Latin American and Caribbean music usually rapped and sung in Spanish, English, and Spanglish (a slang combination of Spanish and English).

Other countries in North America are also contributing to the hip-hop dialogue. Canada is represented every time the successful hip-hop artist Drake releases a composition. He uses one beat maker, named 40 (Noah Shebib), on all his compositions. As of this writing, 105 of their compositions have entered the *Billboard* Hot 100 charts in America.

Cuba has a thriving hip-hop scene called *rap cubano*. The Dominican Republic absorbed the music of Puerto Rico, New York, Boston, and Miami for its homegrown *rap Dominicano* that emerged in 2006. Haiti weighs in with *rap Kreyol*. Mexican beat makers create songs that are labeled *Chicano rap*. El Salvador, in Central America, has had its own rap artists dating back to the early 1990s.

SOUTH AMERICA

Argentina, Bolivia, Chile, Columbia, Ecuador, Paraguay, Peru, Uruguay, and Venezuela are the nine South American countries whose local hip-hop scenes fall within the label of Latin hip-hop. Debuting around the mid 1990s, the beat making has mimicked and kept up with the techniques of American beat makers.

Hip-hop in Brazil began in Sao Paolo before it spread to Rio De Janeiro and almost every other large Brazilian city. America's west coast and southern beat making techniques are the staple beneath rapping about racial and economic issues.

AUSTRALIA

Australian hip-hop began as a response to seeing British hip-hop artists on television in the early 1980s. By the late 1980s, Sound Unlimited Posse became the first hip-hop group signed to a major label. Successful Australian hip-hop artists are of Anglo heritage, and have received crossover appeal into the American market, such as Iggy Azalea and the Kid Laroi.

Indigenous Australian rappers, however, remain true to using hip-hop as a platform to speak about racial injustices and discrimination. Although these artists are not afforded the same level of support as their commercial counterparts, artists like Brothablack, the South West Syndicate, Briggs, and MC Daniel Rankine (Trials) reflect a more accurate sense of indigenous Australian life.

ACTIVITIES CHAPTER 12

Production

Create your own beat. Now is the opportunity to focus on your preferred global hip-hop artists and compositions, and their stylistic elements.

1. Choose an artist from the listening exercises. Use the virtual instruments in your DAW to create a beat and rap that sounds like the hip-hop production style of that global region.
2. Choose a global region. Research the producers of that global region, and identify what features contribute to its distinct character. Use your DAW to create a beat and rap that sounds like their specific production styles.

PART IV

Hip-Hop Production Techniques

The primary focus of this book is to reveal the complex nature of one of the most popular musical art forms of the late twentieth and early twenty-first centuries. It is not a simple art form, but a complex folk music being woven together by modern-day troubadours who wield beats instead of guitars.

There are two critical parts to this music: beats and vocals. But making records is also about sonic "vision." It's not only what rappers and singers are saying that is received by the listening population, but how they say it, how it is recorded, how it is processed, how it is mixed, and how it is mastered. "Hip-Hop Production Techniques" will serve as the "finishing touches" section, presenting vocal production, DAW creativity, and music mixing as necessary concepts for the creative person who wants to produce hip-hop.

CHAPTER 13

Vocal Production

Vocal production has been at the forefront of hip-hop's ability to communicate to its audience since "Rapper's Delight." Hip-hop vocal productions have come a long way since three guys rapped, one after another, and were probably minimally coached.

Thinking of producing vocals in a simple and non "professional audio" way, it is something like recording a voice message on your phone. You want to get your voice sounding right so people believe you are genuinely interested in the fact that you are not available to answer the phone. The tone has to be right, the articulation needs to be clear, and the attitude needs to be in tune with the mood you want to set.

The rappers in the Sugarhill Gang had to also listen to their recorded voices, critique them, and then rerecord parts that could help them connect with their audience. "Rapper's Delight" was meant to entice the audience to dance.

The social commentary of the "The Message" (1982) needed a different, more gritty beat for its lone vocalist, Melle Mel, but the sonic vision similarly presented the vocalist in the center of the speakers, not panned to the left, not panned to the right.

As minimal as hip-hop might seem to the untrained ear, a huge percentage of successful vocals in hip-hop have been recorded in a more "professional audio" way, with conventional recording techniques by trained audio engineers.

Hip-hop has moved from the lone vocalist in the center of the speakers to many more varied approaches as the recordings have become more complex. Listeners are offered a wide variety of listening experiences created by producers and mixing engineers that include multiple locations in the stereo field as well as multiple rappers and/or multiple singers.

A great many beat makers are not well versed in the nuance of producing vocalists, so they will either leave the rappers and singers to their own devices, or bring in a seasoned vocal producer.

Vocal producing evolved from vocal coaching, which focused more on posture, pitch, and articulation. The vocal producer takes into account those characteristics of the human vocal instrument and also possesses a skill set that understands microphone choices, recording environments, preamplifiers, compressors, equalizers, and DAW editing tools and plug-ins.

Professional vocal producers, a role exemplified by Atlanta-based Kuk Harrell in the first decade of the twenty-first century, turn the emotional recordings of artists like Rihanna and Justin Bieber into platinum performances that connect with the entire world.

Focal points for a hip-hop vocal producer are pitch, emotion, and timing, which are collectively known as "flow."

PITCH

The *modal register,* or *chest voice,* is a technical designation for our speaking voice. Each person can perform a range of notes with their chest voice. The upper harmonic structure of the notes we speak or sing gives each of us our own unique tone or *timbre.*

The notes we articulate vibrate at certain frequencies. We call our aural perception of these vibrations the *pitch* of the sound.

Human voices are divided up by range into three main types for men (bass, baritone, tenor) and three main types for women (alto, mezzo-soprano, soprano).

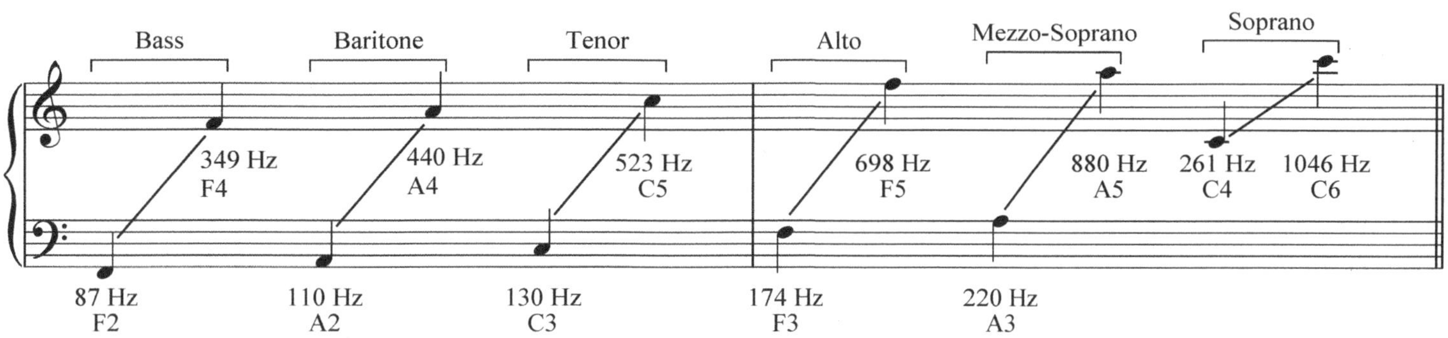

FIG. 13.1. Typical Vocal Ranges

Male rappers are predominantly tenors or baritones and female rappers are predominantly altos. All three rappers on "Rapper's Delight" (Wonder Mike, Big Bank Hank, and Master Gee) are tenors whose spoken pitches are vibrating closely above and below B3 (246 Hz). Drake's singing performance on "One Dance" moves mostly between A♭3 (207 Hz) and E♭3 (155 Hz), placing him at the lower end of the tenor vocal range but squarely in the middle of baritone note ranges. The gruff stylizations of rappers like the Notorious B.I.G. and Rick Ross provide a blend of tenor and baritone pitches, but they are not bass vocalists.

"Whatta Man" by Salt-N-Pepa ft. En Vogue (1993) is being rapped above and below the tonic frequency G4 (392 Hz). Other female rap legends like Queen Latifah, Monie Love, MC Lyte, YoYo, Rage, Lil' Kim, and Foxy Brown all deliver their rhymes within alto note ranges. "Your Love" by Nicki Minaj (2010) moves between B3 (246 Hz) and E4 (329 Hz), placing her performance on that song in the middle of the alto range.

EMOTION

The *emotion* of the human voice in a rap performance is one of the prime features that pulls a listener in. From the deadpan blasé of Mase's 1997 hit "Feel So Good," to the emotional buildup delivered by Eminem in his 2002 hit "Lose Yourself," to the contrasting vocal performance and ad-lib vocal on "Panda" by Desiigner (2015), the emotional content of a rap delivery can make or break even the best beat maker's instrumental.

Emotion is a very personal space for a rapper, but there are noticeable concepts a vocal producer can help with that add to the character of a rap or sung performance.

- *Pitch variation:* Where the notes go up and down a scale for emphasis within a line. This can be heard in each of the three performances on "Rapper's Delight."
- *Groans:* Where the notes are pulled up from the *glottal* register—the lowest notes each vocal type can produce. With a groan, the slide into the fundamental note is usually so fast that the rapper sounds like their voice has a sandpaper quality to it. An example of an artist using groans to his advantage is "Get at Me Dog" by DMX (1998), or the chorus and bridge performance on "In da Club" by 50 Cent (2003), or the Weeknd's vocal delivery on "Low Life" by Future (2016).
- *Moans:* Where the notes descend from the fundamental note into the glottal register. The slide from the fundamental is usually slow and audible. You can hear this vocal anomaly on "Empire State of Mind" by Jay-Z ft. Alicia Keys (2009), or "Bodak Yellow (Money Moves)" by Cardi B (2017). The descending nature of English provides a great opportunity for this device to be used in vocal performances. Consider that vocal inflection in French ascends at the end of each phrase, and you can imagine how difficult it was for French rappers to create a "flow" that resonated well with their audiences.
- *Cries:* Cries move the rap vocalist up into the register above the chest voice. The *falsetto* or *head voice* can be ascended into or descended down from for effective vocal cries. "Trap Queen" by Fetty Wap (2014) is a great example of a rapper using the cries throughout the entire composition. Vocal crying is another one of

the innovations in modern hip-hop that, although subtle, has quickly become a signature for artists exploring pitch and timing variations for vocal performance.

PANNING

When you are listening to a recording, you are listening with two ears. The left ear is listening to a speaker or earbud on the left of your listening position, and the right ear is listening to a speaker or earbud on the right of your listening position. This is called the *stereo field*. Within the stereo field, a mix engineer can place a vocal to the left, to the right, to the center, or anywhere in between those three positions using the pan potentiometer (pan pot) feature contained on all audio consoles and DAWs.

There is no center speaker in the stereo field, so the center position exists because of an identical arrival time from the left and the right speakers to the left and right ears. The phenomenon of audio appearing centered between a left and right location is called the *phantom image*.

From the beginning, rappers were panned to the center of the stereo field, as you can hear in each performance on "Rapper's Delight."

In the audio recording (at https://www.halleonard.com/mylibrary), the lead vocal is presented in the center of the stereo field with one phrase repeated four times.

Audio 13.1. Lead Vocal in Center

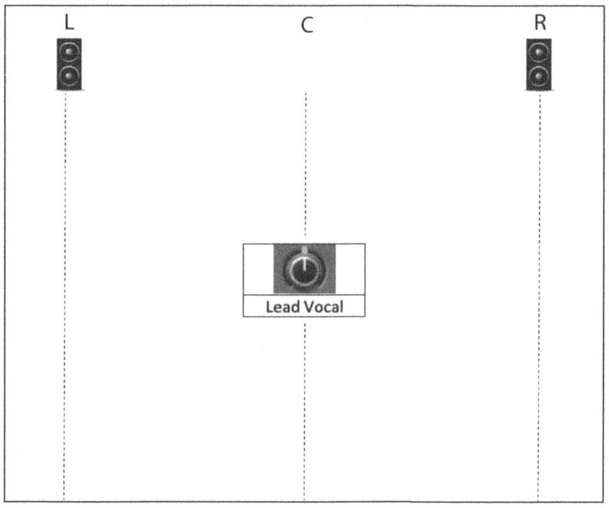

FIG. 13.2. Lead Vocal in Center

Performing the rap a second time and panning both to the center of the stereo field creates a doubled vocal that adds emphasis to the rap, even though it skews articulation slightly. On "Dear Mama" by 2Pac (1995), you can hear that not only has he doubled the vocal but he is also not rapping in complete unison. He creates harmonic dissonance by moving the pitch of his second vocal above the pitch of his main vocal. This doubling with harmonic dissonance became a unique signature for 2Pac that few rappers have successfully emulated. Doubling in the center is done frequently, but most rappers prefer a tighter unison with their doubles.

Audio 13.2 Single Vocal Followed by Lead Doubled In the Center

In the audio, the lead vocal is presented in the center of the stereo field with one phrase repeated four times. The lead vocal is joined on the third and fourth phrases by a lead double.

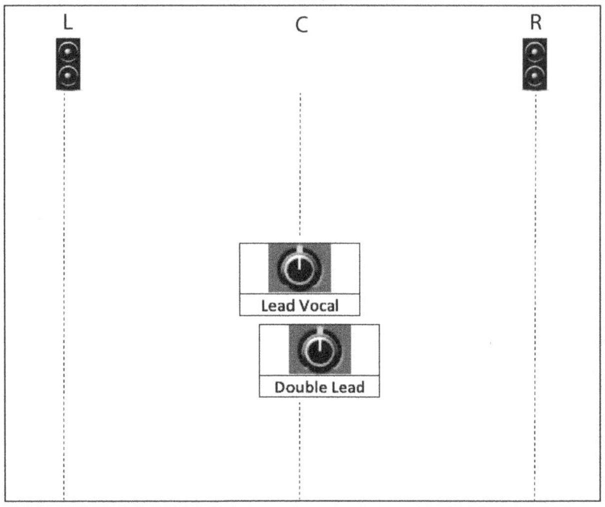

FIG. 13.3. Doubled Vocal in Center (Double Slightly Off Center)

Rappers will also split voices to two sides. This is usually done to add a differentiation between the verse and the chorus. "Wait (The Whisper Song)" by the Ying Yang Twins (2005) is an example of this chorus approach. The center vocal joins and drops out so that both a two-vocal and a three-vocal chorus can be heard.

Audio 13.3 Split Double Joined by Center Lead Vocal

In the audio, the lead vocal is presented as a spread double on the left and right of the stereo field with one phrase repeated four times. The spread double is joined on the third and fourth phrases by a centered lead vocal.

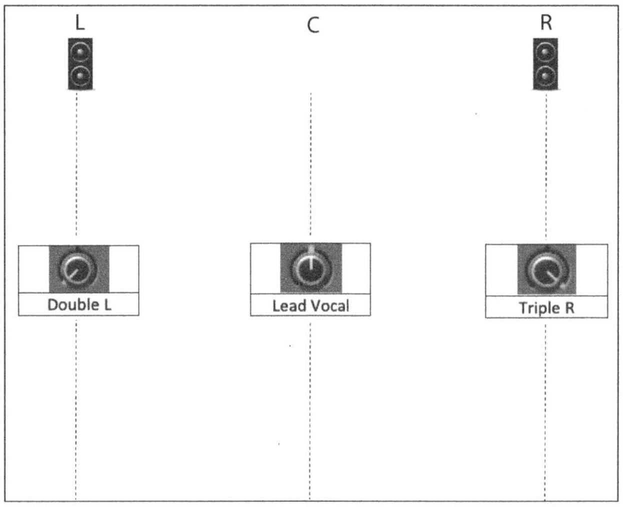

FIG. 13.4. Split-Wide Vocals: Left, Center, and Right

Singers on rap records use center, doubled center, and split-wide techniques for their sections in the record.

Choruses sound even thicker when you double the left and double the right vocals, in a three-part harmony. For instance, your singer would perform four identical tonic phrases, then four identical phrases for the third harmony above the melody, and then four identical phrases for the fifth harmony above the melody, for a total of twelve performed vocal tracks in your chorus. Six of those vocals go to the left, six go to the right.

The result is a thick harmonic and chorus-like blend that is spread wide across the stereo field. "I'll Be Missing You" by Puff Daddy ft. Faith Evans and 112 (1997) is a classic composition that explored this layering concept. "Happy" by Pharrell Williams (2013) and "Despacito" by Luis Fonsi ft. Daddy Yankee (2017) are two other great examples of this vocal formation.

Audio 13.4 Vocal Harmony Stacks

In the audio, the background part is presented as a spread double, three-part harmony, singing a two-note phrase repeated eight times. The first and second phrases contain three harmony notes on the left and three harmony notes on the right. The third and fourth phrases double the existing notes resulting in six harmony notes on the left and six harmony notes on the right. The four-phrase sequence is then repeated and joined by a centered lead vocal.

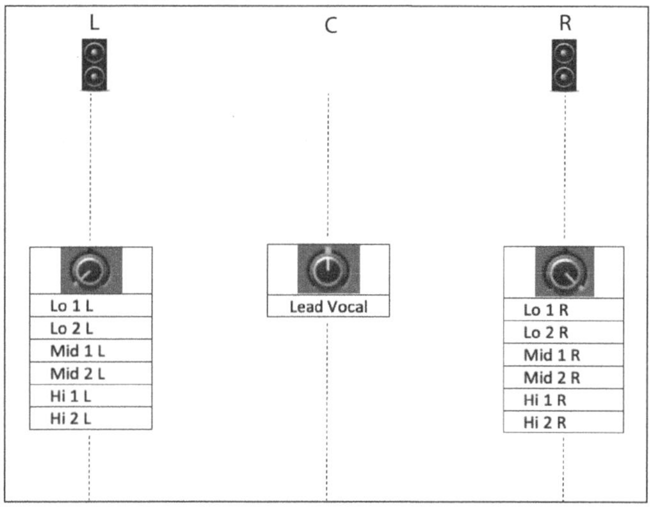

FIG. 13.5. Vocal Harmony Stacks

Hype tracks add a whole other layer of interest in a hip-hop composition. A hype track is the equivalent of a second rapper on stage whose job it is to get the audience excited about listening to the performance. Often, the rapper in the hype track will yell aggressively, like on "Panda," but hype tracks have also been known to be laid back, like Puff Daddy's work on "Juicy" by the Notorious B.I.G.

The *ad-lib* track is a track that reinforces lyrics by mouthing sound effects or contrapuntal phrases meant to move the storyline along. You can hear an ad-lib vocal alternately talking, shouting, and singing through the rap verses in "Trap Queen" by Fetty Wap.

The panning position for hype tracks and ad-lib tracks can be anywhere in the stereo field that does not interfere with the lead vocal delivery.

EQ

EQ is short for *equalization* and describes devices that modify the frequency response of audio events. One way that hip-hop vocal producers use equalizers is to turn the controls or move the sliders to see if they like the affect it has on the vocal. On parametric equalizers, there is a level control, a center frequency select, and a bandwidth select (that can raise or lower frequencies around the center frequency).

Common Parameters for a Parametric Equalizer

Low Pass	Attenuates frequencies *above* a selected frequency
Low Gain	±20 Hz to 125 Hz
Low-Mid Gain	±125 Hz to 500 Hz (slight attenuation around 300 Hz for vocals)
Mid Gain	± 500 Hz to 2 kHz
High-Mid Gain	± 2 kHz to 8 kHz (slight attenuation near 3 kHz for vocals)
High Gain	± 8 kHz to 20 kHz (slight boost near 10 kHz for vocals)
High Pass	Attenuates frequencies *below* a selected frequency

Each frequency will also contain a bandwidth adjust, also called Q. The Q is the width of frequencies that will be raised or lowered around the center frequency and is determined by the formula f_0/f_2-f_1 where f_0 is the center frequency, f_2 is the frequency above the center frequency and f_1 is the frequency below the center frequency).

Another way to apply EQ is to use the tempered scale when you want to boost or attenuate frequency response. This technique has been used by professional recording, mixing, and mastering engineers since the early 1960s to add or subtract focus of differing parts of the frequency spectrum using an approach that emphasizes the known pitches of equal temperament. Basically, you can EQ your song based on the key of its tonic frequency. This accelerates the artistic use of equalization by lessening the guesswork of which frequencies help, or hurt, your sonic vision.

Let's say we are working on a track in the style of "Big Poppa" by the Notorious B.I.G. (1994), and it is in the key of A minor. Well, immediately all the A's are frequencies that you can potentially *boost* (turn up) or *attenuate* (turn down). Those ten frequencies would be:

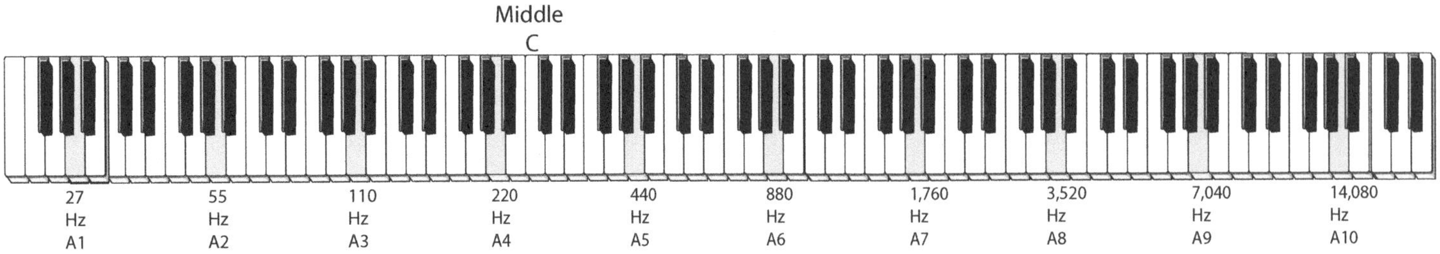

FIG. 13.6. Frequency of Every A Note

Add to that the third harmonic of the harmonic series for each note, which is a perfect fifth above the tonic, or E, and you have ten other frequencies to work with:

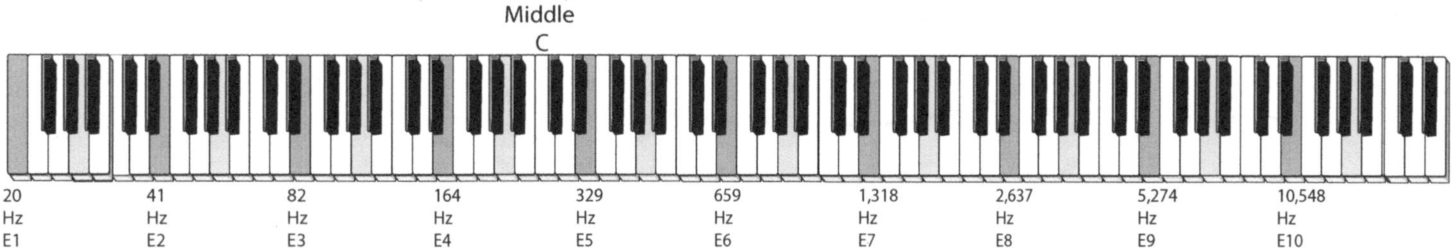

FIG. 13.7. Frequency of Every E Note (A also shown)

Now, let's add the fifth harmonic of the harmonic series, which is a major third above the tonic, or C♯, and we will have ten more frequencies:

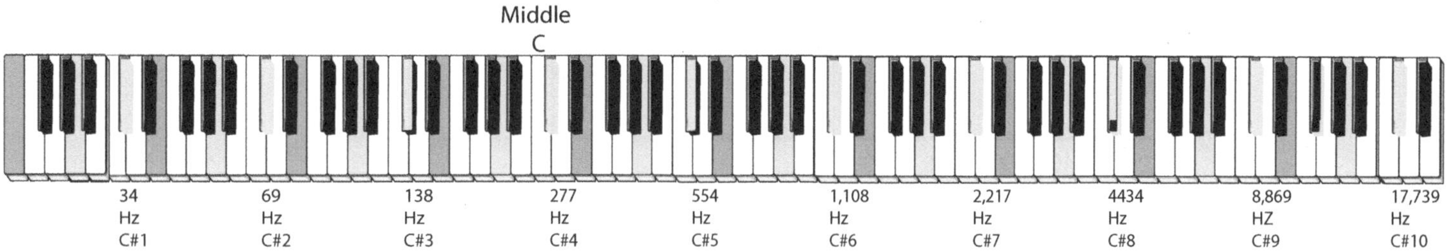

FIG. 13.8. Frequency of Every C♯ Note (A and E also shown)

So, as you're working on this composition in A, in the recording or mixing process, you have already located thirty frequencies that can address any problems you may have in the low, low-mid, mid, high-mid, or high frequencies. For instance, if the vocal needs more body, that is in the 200 Hz range. Your tonic in A is 220 cycles, so boosting that frequency would be more efficient than relying on the Q (the width of frequencies adjusted around a center frequency) at 200 Hz to address the lack of body. Another example would be if your female singer's voice in the sample is too harsh. You will be informed by the *Equal-Loudness Contours (ISO 226:2003)* chart that frequencies near 3 kHz are harsh to the ear. The frequency 3,520 Hz is the tonic A, and turning this abrasive frequency down a bit will make a difference in what you are hearing.

This is a simple idea that when practiced can speed up the hip-hop workflow immensely. You will also need to study the Equal-Loudness Contours chart for an understanding of how people perceive sound pressure. That chart gives you an idea of how humans perceive sound. Because hip-hop can communicate, minimally, with just a vocal and a beat, equalization is an important part of exciting the ears. Each performance in the composition can be felt by the listener as having a maximum amount of interesting sonic information. Used properly, to highlight certain frequencies and to lowlight other frequencies, it will have your vocals and instruments sitting in great shape relative to each other.

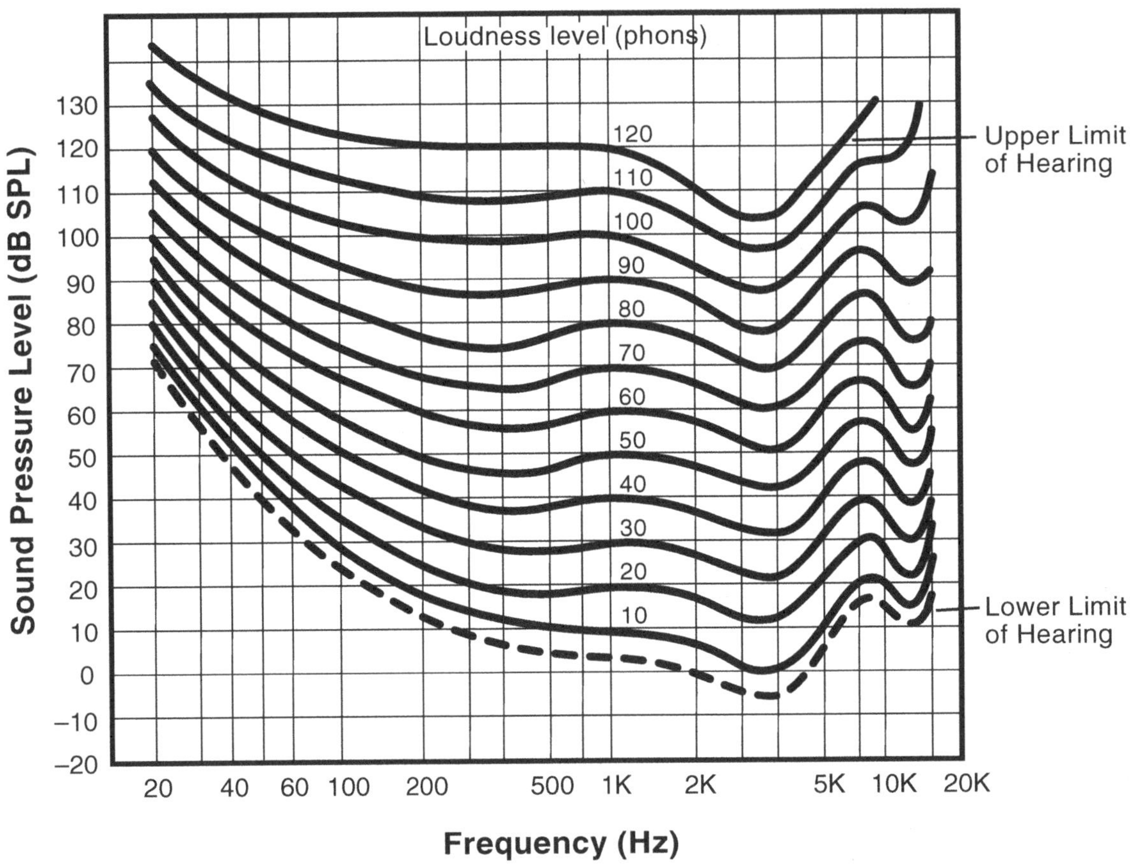

FIG. 13.9. Equal Loudness Contours (ISO 226:2003)

If you must use EQ when initially recording your rapper or vocalist (as opposed to during mixing), I recommend that it be slight. Even very slight processing can result in a duller sounding vocal. It is relatively easy to contour a performance with additional equalization adjusts on the playback side. Once you become more experienced, if you feel like you have a great chain of devices for vocals and your ears have gotten used to the recording process, then—and only then—would I suggest printing with EQ curves that are not slight.

LEVEL

Level refers to a measured voltage ratio of audio signals, or rather, how loud each part is relative to others. The loudest instrument in hip-hop records is usually the rap, so you can hear the story. The next instrument to dominate the audio spectrum has historically been the kick drum, followed by the bass. I say "historically" because you must remember, we are dealing with an art form that challenges all norms, even its own.

In "Rapper's Delight," the bass line was at a prominent level. In "My Adidas" by Run-DMC (1986), the Oberheim DMX kick drum and snare dominated the beat behind the vocals. "Bring the Noise" by Public Enemy (1988) used the drum loop from "Funky Drummer" by James Brown and the J.B.'s (1970) as its focal point slightly lower than the vocals.

Now why do I mention these second-loudest focuses in a chapter discussing vocal production? Because the loudest part (the rap) is only loud relative to the second, third, fourth (and so on) loudest things in the record. To identify the ideal level for the rap, you need to understand the best levels of all the other instruments in the composition.

Most of the time, these relationships are sorted out when the record is being mixed. But even during the recording process, the rapper needs to hear a good instrumental relationship in their headphones so that they can perform properly.

Your DAW measures digital amplitude (volume) in dBFS (decibels relative to full scale). The Society of Motion Picture and Television Engineers (SMPTE) defines –20 dBFS as 0 VU (volume units: the analog measurement of amplitude). Levels above –20 dBFS could contain peak information that adds distortion to your vocal recording. That said, pushing a vocal on its recording track to about –6 dBFS is about where digital distortion can ruin your vocal recording.

COMPRESSION

One of the most useful devices in hip-hop vocal production, after the microphone, is the compressor, because the compressors can aid in the quest to keep vocal levels under control with no added peak information. Compressors are simply automatic gain-reduction devices. They can be used to even out parts of a vocal performance that stick out too much.

Recording compression is best if used minimally, and not recorded to your recording medium. Gain reduction should not exceed –3 dB.

Some rappers and vocalists may have poor microphone technique where they constantly move away from the best recording distance to the microphone. Performing in front of the optimal microphone position is called "on-axis," and anywhere to the side or too far away from this point is considered off-axis. Remaining on-axis to the microphone will yield the best vocal recording, and the best triggering of your compressor.

Common Compressor Parameters

- **Input.** The level of the signal as it enters your compressor.
- **Threshold.** The point at which your vocalist will trigger the compressor to move from a 1:1 ratio (which is no compression) to the dialed-in ratio. Your threshold will vary in order to achieve the proper amount of gain reduction at peak level, but once you set it, try your best to get your vocalist to use proper microphone technique.
- **Ratio.** Average ratios of output attenuation for a hip-hop vocal performance should be 3:1 or 4:1. At a 3:1 ratio, every 3 dB over the threshold would result in 1 dB of output over the threshold. At a 4:1 ratio, every 4 dB over the threshold would result in 1 dB of output over the threshold.

- **Gain Reduction.** This is the amount that a vocal is turned down once it hits the threshold level. The average gain reduction for a hip-hop vocal performance should be no more than –6 dB. Any more than this can be heard by the listener as an unnatural lowering of the vocal, which is antithetical to the nature of natural vocal performance.
- **Attack.** The amount of time it takes for the compressor to turn down the portion of the performance that is too loud. The attack time should be fast for hip-hop vocal performances, between 20 and 800 μs (microseconds).
- **Release.** The amount of time it takes for the compressor to revert back to a 1:1 state. The release time should be medium so that any "pumping" from the release of the compressor is minimized. Medium is about 10 to 20 ms (milliseconds).
- **Knee.** The ability of the compressor to sweep from 1:1 ratio to the goal ratio, with the threshold point in between. A *hard knee* is immediate compression at the threshold. A *soft knee* is a logarithmic slope toward the target ratio. I prefer a hard knee for most hip-hop vocal performances.
- **Output.** Compressors are "attenuators"; they turn sound lower. The output adjustment gives you the ability to turn up the overall "turned down" version of the vocal performance.

Be careful: some compressors have automatic gain makeup, which will turn the compressor's output gain up the more it compresses. This is a great feature, but if misunderstood, you might overuse it and over-compress your vocal.

These are the main techniques that a hip-hop vocal producer would focus on as they record and mix a rapper or singer. Of course, the bag of tricks doesn't stop here. Processing vocal performances and creating artificial textures are in the domain of audio editing, which many vocal producers exercise via their command of the DAW and specialized third-party plug-ins. These sorts of tools did not exist in 1979, but as they have appeared on the market, hip-hop producers have purchased them, explored them, and found creative uses for them that have surpassed their intended use.

ACTIVITIES CHAPTER 13

Listening

We have already listened to these compositions for the musical elements. Now, it's time to listen to them with a focus on the vocal performances. Listen to each song and make note of the following parameters:

1. Is the vocal natural, nasal, or breathy sounding?
2. How many vocals are performing in each section?
3. How are the lead vocals, ad-lib vocals, and/or background vocals panned in the composition?
4. What are the highest and lowest notes in the range of the lead vocalist?
5. Identify the types of sound processing used on the vocals in this production. Do you hear Auto-Tune, distortion, reverb, or delays? If you produced these vocals, would you have used the same approach or offered the vocalist different options?
    - "Trap Queen" by Fetty Wap (2015)
    - "Panda" by Desiigner (2015)
    - "Low Life" by Future ft. the Weeknd (2016)
    - "One Dance" by Drake (2016)
    - "Bodak Yellow (Money Moves)" by Cardi B (2017)
    - "Despacito" by Luis Fonsi ft. Daddy Yankee (2017)
    - "Sicko Mode" by Travis Scott (2018)
    - "I Like It" by Cardi B ft. Bad Bunny and J Balvin (2018)
    - "Old Town Road" by Lil Nas X (2019)
    - "Truth Hurts" by Lizzo (2019)

Production

Create your own sound-alike:

1. **Making the beat.** Use the virtual instruments in your DAW to create a sound alike of one of the compositions on our list. You must try your best to make every instrument sound exactly like the instruments in the composition you have chosen.
2. **Rapping and/or singing to the beat.** Record the vocal performances from your chosen composition into your instrumental sound-alike. This can be your voice or someone that you produce. You are trying to match the performances, timbres and processing of the chosen composition. (Note: Push through any apprehensions you may have about you or your vocalist's abilities. This vocal exercise is meant to help you better understand how to communicate about vocal production techniques within hip-hop songs.)

CHAPTER 14

A Creative Revolution—DAWs and Plug-Ins: 2001 to Present

Listening: DAW-Based Hip-Hop

- "Chopped N Skrewed" by T-Pain ft. Ludacris (2008)
- "Broccoli" by D.R.A.M. ft. Lil Yachty (2016)
- "I'm the One" by DJ Khaled ft. Justin Bieber, Quavo, Chance the Rapper, and Lil Wayne (2017)
- "1-800-273-8255" by Logic ft. Alessia Cara & Khalid (2017)
- "Bodak Yellow (Money Moves)" by Cardi B (2017)

The rebellious technical innovations in hip-hop did not cease with the advent of the twenty-first century; they only accelerated. The vocal performances of Akon, Lil Wayne, T-Pain, Kanye West, and Drake were all processed using digital plug-ins such as Antares's Auto-Tune and Celemony's Melodyne to create synthetic-sounding vocal performances full of integrated human emotion.

Each successive generation has figured out how to use emerging technological devices as creative tools in ways that they weren't necessarily designed for. If you listen to the best of the young lions, you'll hear soulfulness—not in the notes that they play, but in the heart and soul that looks at what is and says, "What could be?" What could the turntable be? What could live band production be? What could a drum machine be? What could the MIDI protocol be? What could a sampler be? What could a DAW be? And what could a plug-in be?

Let's start by peering inside the DAW. At the most successful levels, a large percentage of hip-hop is mixed in Pro Tools. Many of the productions are not created in Pro Tools however. Logic, Reason, FL Studio, and Ableton Live are used for the creative portion of beat making. The MPC (and its MIDI controller counterparts, the MPD and Maschine) is also still a functioning tool set for seasoned hip-hop producers, but a younger generation of beat makers is moving more toward full software packages instead of integrated hardware and software.

THE DAW: DIGITAL AUDIO WORKSTATION

The Digital Audio Workstation changed the workflow for hip-hop producers at the turn of the twenty-first century. DAWs offer more to the producer than the simple process of recording audio signals. They allow for quick editing and the alteration of files in new, and seemingly unlimited, ways that were not available with simple samplers and sequencers and splicing tape. Techniques like automatic tuning and elastic audio allow the producer to create new rhythms, tunings, and timbres using plug-in software tools that modify recorded audio.

Time Bases

Track *time bases* in DAWs provide two primary time scales for you to track the material in your hip-hop composition.

- **Absolute Time.** A sample-based constant absolute position in the DAW that can be read as HH:MM:SS:mm or as samples/sec. Common sample rates in hip-hop are 44.1 kHz and 48 kHz.
- **Relative Time.** A tempo-based bar/beat position in the DAW that can be read as PPQN (pulses per quarter note). MIDI requires the composite number 24 as a minimum PPQN, but software packages such as Pro Tools and Logic use 960 PPQN, which is the 40th multiple of 24.

The majority of current hip-hop productions are music sequencer based and use relative time (bars/beats) to keep track of the sequences and loops in a composition. Setting the correct tempo is the first thing that a beat maker needs to do when creating a song in a DAW.

Tempo Mapping

In chapter 1, I showed you a formula that used milliseconds as an absolute measurement of time and the duration of one bar as being relative to different tempos (bpm).

$$60{,}000 \text{ ms} \times 4 \text{ beats}/1 \text{ bar in milliseconds} = \text{bpm}$$

To refresh, 60,000 ms is the result of multiplying the smallest increment of time per second, the millisecond, by 60 to get milliseconds per minute.

$$1{,}000 \text{ ms} \times 60 \text{ s} \times 4 \text{ beats}/1 \text{ bar in milliseconds} = \text{bpm}$$

Our DAWs use samples as the smallest increment of absolute time per second. A more accurate tempo can be mapped using samples instead of milliseconds.

$$48{,}000 \text{ samples} \times 60 \text{ s} \times 4 \text{ beats}/1 \text{ bar in samples} = \text{bpm}$$

Or, since we have a few different sample rates to choose from, this is the formula for tempo mapping:

$$SR \times 60 \times NB/NS = \text{bpm}$$

Where SR is: the Sample Rate in samples per second
60 is: the number of seconds in a minute
NB is: the number of beats in your bars, and
NS is: the number of samples in your selected bars

Here are three examples with three different sample rates and bar lengths. Let's calculate the tempo of each one. We will divide the number of samples in each selection into the sample rate per minute times the number of beats per bar.

1. A one-bar phrase (4 beats) at 96 kHz sampling rate

$$96{,}000 \times 60 \times 4 \text{ beats}/280{,}976 = 82 \text{ bpm}$$

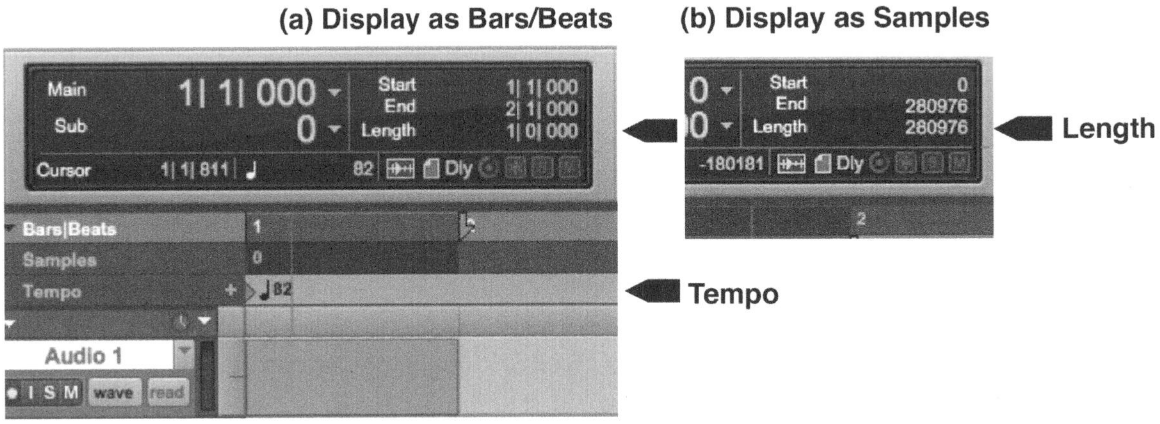

FIG. 14.1. One-Bar Sample, Displaying Length in (a) Bar Length and (b) Sample Length

2. A two-bar phrase (8 beats) at 48 kHz sampling rate:

$$48{,}000 \times 60 \times 8 \text{ beats}/209{,}455 = 110 \text{ bpm}$$

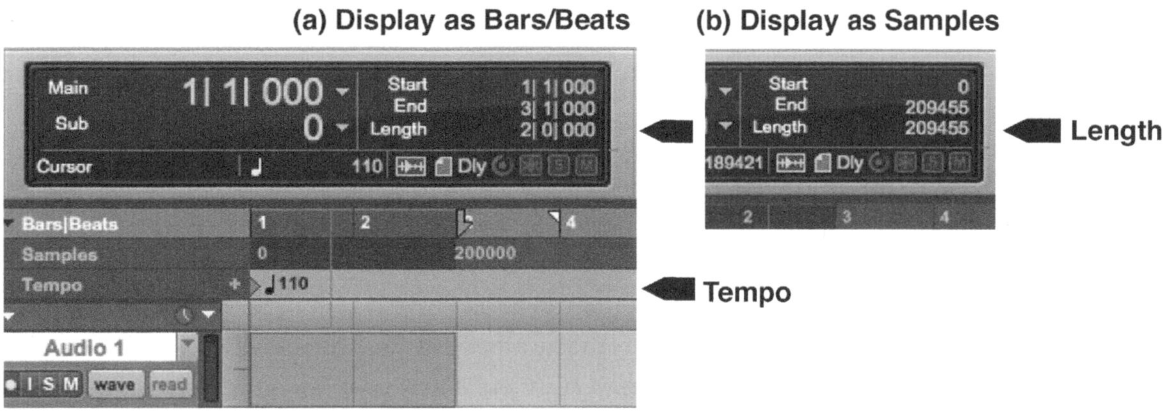

FIG. 14.2. Two-Bar Sample

3. An eight-bar (32 beats) phrase at 44.1 kHz sampling rate

$$44{,}100 \times 60 \times 32 \text{ beats}/717{,}559 = 118 \text{ bpm}$$

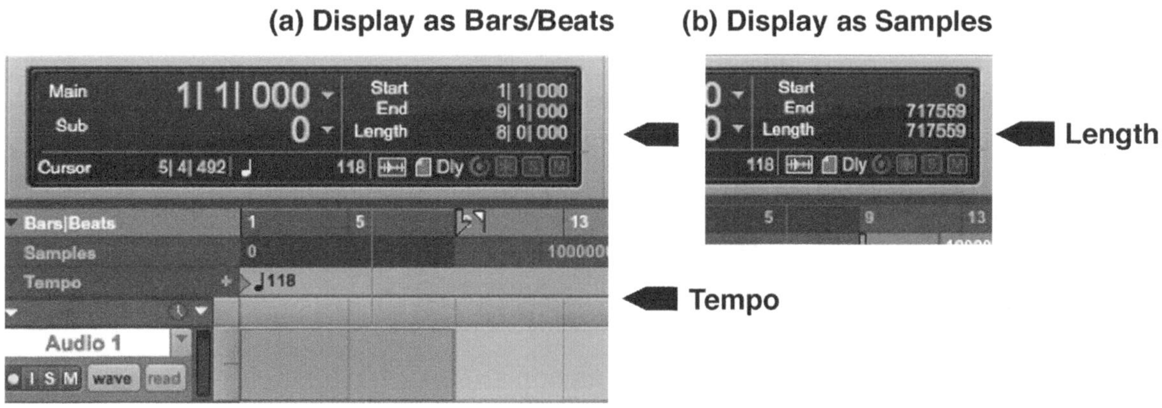

FIG. 14.3. Eight-Bar Sample

A fine-tuned understanding of sample position for a beat maker can make time compression and expansion an effortless tool for innovative creations.

Samples Per Pulse

Because of the consistency of MIDI and music sequencing, beat makers do not use tempo mapping. There is a quirky thing about dialing in one tempo in MIDI and tempo maps. If you create a beat at 110.0 bpm, and tempo map the kick drum at the beginning of every bar, there is a good chance you will get a range of tempos near 110.0 but not 110.0. This is due to a few things:

1. where the transient in the kick was detected
2. the serial nature of MIDI, and
3. the number of samples available per pulse.

If the kick drum transient is detected even one sample from the absolute sample position for 110 bpm, the tempo revealed will adjust slightly. Also, MIDI moves in a stream a 31.25 kb per second, which is a lower resolution than your DAW's sample rate. And finally, each pulse has a range of samples that it can actually occur before it becomes the next pulse.

$$SR \times 60s/bpm = \text{samples per beat}$$

For instance, one beat at a 48 kHz sampling rate and a tempo of 60 bpm would have 48,000 samples per beat.

$$48{,}000 \text{ samples} \times 60s/60 \text{ bpm} = 48{,}000 \text{ samples per beat}$$

Divide one beat (a quarter note) by the number of pulses per quarter note (PPQN) that your DAW uses for MIDI resolution, and you will reveal the number of samples per pulse.

$$(SR \times 60 \text{ s/bpm})/PPQN = \text{samples per pulse.}$$

So, one beat at a 48 kHz sampling rate and a tempo of 60 bpm would have 50 available sample locations per pulse because many of the most popular DAWs use a 960 PPQN.

$$(48{,}000 \text{ samples} \times 60 \text{ s/60 bpm})/960 \text{ PPQN} = 50 \text{ (available) sample positions per pulse.}$$

This is an example of the 50 sample tolerance in MIDI at 60 bpm:

Figure 14.4 shows bar 1/beat 2/sub-beat 000 at its absolute time position, which is at 48,000 samples.

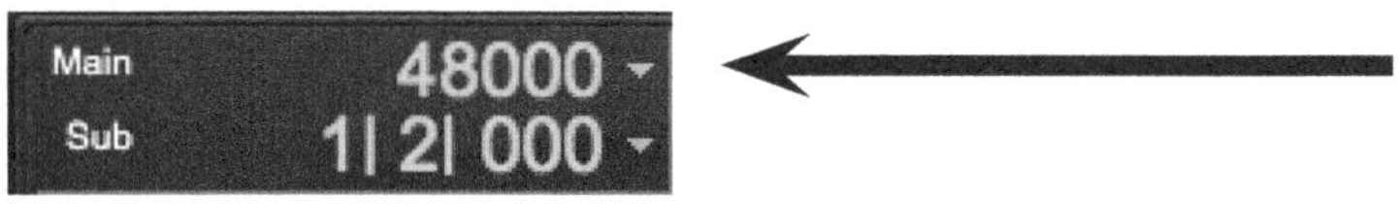

FIG. 14.4. Beat 2 Sub-Beat 000 Quantized at 48,000 Samples (60 bpm)

Figure 14.5 shows bar 1/beat 2/sub-beat 000, 24 samples later, just before it becomes bar 1/beat 2/sub-beat 001. It is still bar 1/beat 2/sub-beat 000.

FIG. 14.5. Last Sample of Beat 2 Sub-Beat 000 within 50 Sample Tolerance Later Than the Quantized Position

Figure 14.6 shows barl/beat 2/sub-beat 001, which is not at the absolute sample position for this sub-beat, but is within the tolerance of this sub-beat.

FIG. 14.6. First Sample of Beat 2 Sub-Beat 001 within 50 Sample Tolerance Earlier Than the Quantized Position

The absolute position for bar 1/beat 2/sub-beat 001 is 48,050 samples, as shown in figure 14.7.

FIG. 14.7. Beat 2 Sub-Beat 001 Quantized at 48,000 Samples (60 bpm)

Which means there are 25 sub-beats prior to the absolute position of bar 1/beat 2/sub-beat 000 as shown in figure 14.8.

FIG. 14.8. Last Sample of Beat 2 Sub-Beat 000 within 50 Sample Tolerance Earlier Than the Quantized Position

The outer edge of tolerance for bar 1/beat 1/sub-beat 959 will be at 47,974 samples, as shown in figure 14.9.

FIG. 14.9. First Sample of Beat 1 Sub-Beat 959 within 50 Sample Tolerance Later Than the Quantized Position

And the absolute time position of bar 1/beat 1/sub-beat 959 is at sample 47,950, as shown in figure 14.10.

FIG. 14.10. Beat 1 Sub-Beat 959 Quantized at 48,000 Samples (60 bpm)

Understanding MIDI against the audio timeline within your DAW at this level of detail makes an effortless task out of editing at the micro level. You can also use this level of detail to program your hip-hop beats in an unquantized fashion like J. Dilla and other avant-garde producers.

Time Compression and Expansion

One of the more interesting features on modern DAWs is time compression and expansion (TCE). It's called Elastic Audio by Digidesign (the original manufacturers of Pro Tools), Flex by Apple, Warp by Ableton, and Stretch by Image-Line.

TCE detects transient information in an audio file. You can lock those detected transients to bar/beat positions relative to the tempo(s) of your DAW session. If you wish to change the tempo, *perceptual coding* is used to add or subtract samples from your audio file. The result is that you can slow audio down or speed audio up with or without pitch changes. This makes it possible to use a wider variety of samples in recordings without needing to change the pitch of either the original sample or the new recording, which opens the doors to many additional creative possibilities.

This DAW functionality effectively chops audio, at the individual sample level, and moves the sliced samples to different positions. The formula for the redistribution of tempo and/or pitch is $f_n = f_0 \times (\sqrt[12]{2})^n$.

There are a few different perceptual coding algorithms:

- **Rhythmic.** Compresses or expands the positions of transient information detected in an audio file by using a larger grain size, which preserves the integrity of *percussive* transient information (e.g., on a kick, snare, or hi-hat track). The chromatic formula, $f_n = f_0 \times (\sqrt[12]{2})^n$, is used to change the tempo only. *The pitch remains the same.*
- **Monophonic.** Compresses or expands the positions of transient information detected in an audio file by using a very small grain size which preserves the integrity of *simple harmonic* audio information (e.g., on a vocal or bass track). The chromatic formula, $f_n = f_0 \times (\sqrt[12]{2})^n$, is used to change the tempo only. *The pitch remains the same.*
- **Polyphonic.** Compresses or expands the positions of transient information detected in an audio file by using a medium grain size which preserves the integrity of *complex harmonic* audio information. This is the "go-to" time compression algorithm than can be used for a wide variety of audio, from drums to full songs. The chromatic formula, $f_n = f_0 \times (\sqrt[12]{2})^n$, is used to change the tempo only. *The pitch remains the same.*
- **Varispeed.** Compresses or expands the positions of transient information detected in an audio file and follows the chromatic formula, $f_n = f_0 \times (\sqrt[12]{2})^n$, for tempo and pitch changes simultaneously. *These pitch and tempo changes are the same that would occur on a tape machine, turntable, or sampler if they were sped up or slowed down.*

Figure 14.11 shows a two-bar example of "Funky Drummer" at its original tempo, which is 97.4837 bpm, and occupies 217,144 samples.

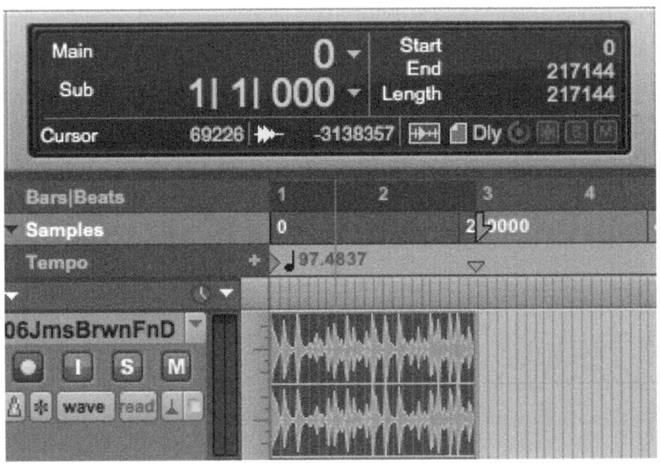

FIG. 14.11. Original One-Bar Phrase: 97.4837 bpm (217,144 Samples)

Figure 14.12 shows the same two-bar phrase polyphonically conformed to 110 bpm. It now occupies 192,436 samples but is still at the same pitch.

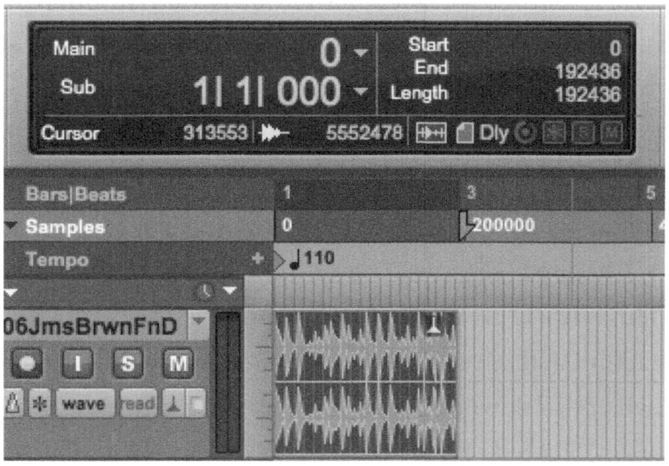

FIG. 14.12. Conforming Original Phrase to 110 bpm (192,436 Samples)

And, figure 14.13 shows the same phrase polyphonically conformed to 90 bpm, it now occupies 235,200 samples and is still at the same pitch.

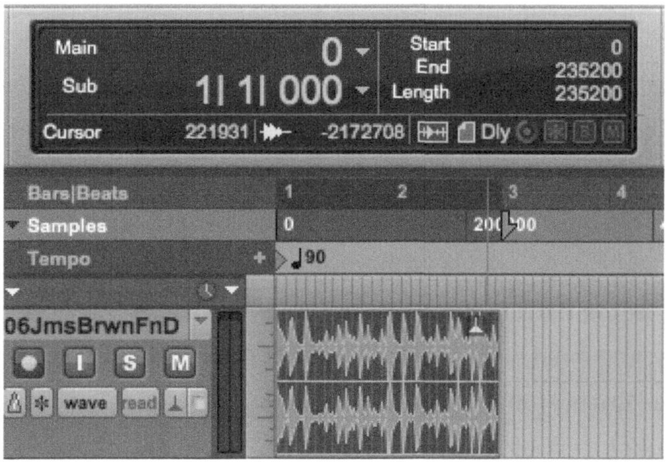

FIG. 14.13. Conforming Original Phrase to 90 bpm (235,200 Samples)

Understanding the TCE tools within your DAW allows you to move samples around much more quickly that you might be able to with a sampler, or by chopping and moving audio. However, I would label it a different creative choice, not a better creative choice. Do not be afraid to experiment with this fundamental feature within your hip-hop compositions.

PLUG-INS

Plug-ins are used to emulate hardware devices that process audio with a wide range of applications. DAW manufacturers and third-party manufacturers have made available dynamic processors (compressors, limiters, expanders, gates, and equalizers), time-based processors (reverbs, delays, phasers, flangers, and chorusers), and file modifiers (tuners, distortion units, transient shapers, and synthetic morphers) that are being heard in hip-hop compositions frequently and with ever-more daring implementation.

Some of the audio-processing staples in the modern hip-hop producer's arsenal are tape slowdown (or speed-up), pitch shifting, automatic tuning, automatic timing, and ambient filtering.

Tape slowdown/speed-up enables you to create an effect of either slowing down to a complete stop or speeding up from a complete stop. This effect can be applied on a single instrument (or voice), a group of instruments, or on the entire composition. The chorus of "Chopped N Skrewed" by T-Pain (2008) contains a tape slowdown on bar 6, beat 4. This is made even more interesting because it is not a smooth slowdown slope like that found in the Pro Tools Audio Suite plug-in called Vari-Fi; it is a stepped slowdown. This type of slowdown feels like there are subtle stutters occurring as the audio slows down. There are a few time-consuming ways to create this effect, but one of the simplest ways is to use the Synchro Arts Effectrix plug-in. A combination of the X-Loop parameter and the Vinyl parameter, adjusted for tempo and length of slowdown, will allow you to create this stunning effect across the entire track.

Pitch shifting enables you to transpose the pitch of any vocal or instrument without changing the speed of the audio. The chromatic formula, $f_n = f_0 \times (\sqrt[12]{2})^n$, is used to define pitch grids (e.g., chromatic, major, and minor scales), track pitch performances, and edit pitch performances. *The tempo remains the same.*

Most DAWs have incorporated a pitch-shifting plug-in within their architecture. A notable third-party plug-in that can pitch shift is Native Instruments' Kontakt. It can sample audio, give you MIDI control, and manipulate pitch without altering the speed of the audio. You can play different keys and hear different pitches, and each pitch will be in the correct tempo with the composition. In order for this to function correctly, you must be in the Wave Editor, select Sync/Slice, and engage the Use Time Machine Pro button. If you want to create MIDI data that plays to a tempo grid, the Grid should be enabled (still in the Wave Editor) and the correct tempo should be dialed in. This effect can be heard in each of the post-choruses in "Chopped N Skrewed" by T-Pain. The lower voice is detuned by a perfect fifth (seven semitones in MIDI language), performing in the correct tempo but altered in pitch.

Automatic tuning continuously tracks the pitch of an incoming sound and compares it to a scale that you can define. Major and minor scales are the primary scale choices by hip-hop producers, but singers can benefit from the pitch subtleties of a chromatic scale. This automatic tuning can be done by DAW plug-ins but the dominant game changer for this technology is Antares Auto-Tune. Developed by Andy Hildebrand as software for processing reflection seismology data in search of oil for Exxon Production Research Company and his co-founded company, Landmark Graphics, Auto-Tune was first heard on "Believe" by Cher (1998). It was met with huge resistance from the music community for its artificial correcting of human pitch. But the debut album *Trouble* by Akon (2004) showed the creative hip-hop community the potential of auto-tuning as a creative vocal tool. Akon signed an artist named T-Pain the following year and, even though he is a very good singer,

T-Pain explored auto-tuning to an even more extreme degree on his debut album, *Rappa Ternt Sanga* (2005), and its lead single, "I'm Sprung." He used the Detune Speed parameter of the plug-in set to fast, and created slightly off pitch performances so that Antares' plug-in would trigger an "artificial" vocal sound. Although some are slight (Khalid) and others are more extreme (Migos), almost all hip-hop performers use some type of automatic tuning when they record vocal performances.

Another extremely popular tuning application is Celemony Melodyne. Melodyne tunes *after* you have recorded your audio. Almost all current major productions in popular music rely on this tuning tool.

It's a time saver that works well to:

- modify the pitch, pitch drift, pitch modulation, position, length, and volume
- shift the formant spectrum
- modify the pitch transition and volume transition between notes
- shift the formant spectrum of transitions between notes
- shift the timing (manually or via macro)
- quantize one track based on the timing of another
- quantize pitch (manually or via macro); transfer melodies from track to track without changing the instrument sound of the destination track; and
- cut, copy, and paste.

The flexibility of this tool has created new offshoots and sub-genres of hip-hop like mumble, where rappers sing and singers rap, almost indistinctly, and everyone is tuned and shifted where they need it to fit the recording. There are so many hip-hop compositions using Melodyne, whether subtly or drastically, that it is impossible to provide "best use" advice for this tool. Suffice it to say, all hip-hop that sounds well-tuned is utilizing Melodyne or Auto-Tune.

Figure 14.14 shows the narrow pitch range of a rapper, in a four-bar rhyme by the artist Ohene from "Scotronixx 2.0" by Dr. Scot Brown ft. Ohene (2020). Notice the various vocal pitches.

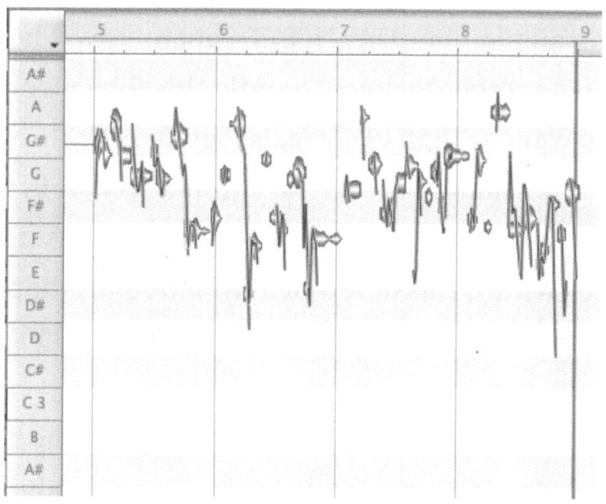

FIG. 14.14. Pitch Range in Ohene's "Scotronixx 2.0" by Dr. Scot Brown ft. Ohene

Figure 14.16 shows a singer's wider pitch range of a two-bar melody from the first verse of "Happy" by Pharrell Williams as recreated by vocalist Joanna Teters. Rapping and singing both occupy notes within the scale of tuning devices. The hip-hop producer can use the tuning tools subtly or harshly to create a wide range of effects on both rappers and singers.

FIG. 14.15. Pitch Range in Pharrell Williams' "Happy"

Of course, the rebellious nature of hip-hop is now even questioning whether using the correct pitch is not something that can be challenged. A good example of the rejection of tuning tools is "Broccoli" by D.R.A.M. ft. Lil Yachty (2016). This is a brilliant deconstruction of perfection in hip-hop. Neither artist is tuned to perfection because the imperfect performances highlight the intoxicating nature of smoking "broccoli" (weed or marijuana).

Automatic timing is used most effectively to automatically edit the timing of one audio signal to line up with the timing of another audio signal. This technique is similar to quantizing but instead aligning to a fixed position along a time grid, you are moving audio to the prescribed time variations of a guide audio file. You can do this job by tediously cutting, moving, and/or pasting audio from one position to another. Or you can use your DAW's TCE capabilities. The Synchro Arts plug-in VocAlign, and its big brother Revoice, handle this job splendidly. Now, you might ask, why would you want to align two vocals together? Or three, or four, or twelve, or thirty-six? Well, this is usually done for background vocals in pop hip-hop compositions. Four individual performances per harmonic note is a standard approach to creating harmonies within the stereo field in a pop hip-hop production. You can also hear this technique throughout the composition "1-800-273-8255" by Logic ft. Alessia Cara & Khalid (2017).

The alignment is done by analyzing the transients in the first audio track, called the *guide*. The analysis of the transients in the second audio track, called the *dub*, then go through a TCE warping to line up similarly positioned transients with the guide track. This can be done on one track at a time in VocAlign or on multiple tracks simultaneously in Revoice.

Mutes and *filters* are used to create dynamics in an otherwise static music bed. These two techniques are use more often than drum fills in modern hip-hop. Muting can be done with your DAW for any instrument. In general, the idea that hip-hop is all about drums has been turned upside down by a generation that has sought its own rebellious approaches to the evolving art form. The result is compositions that mute drums for long periods of time but are still a compelling the target audience to move their bodies to the beat.

Filtering can be done with your native DAW plug-ins or hundreds of third-party plug-ins. The hip-hop producer uses filters and mutes as tension-and-release, within the composition, across different instrumentation groupings. "Bodak Yellow (Money Moves)" by Cardi B (2017) uses a hi-pass filter on its main melody that makes the entrance of the muted drums feel far more dramatic.

Downsampling is another filter-like sound that's useful for hip-hop beat makers. Downsampling removes information from recorded audio and sounds very similar to low pass filtering. But, where low pass filtering is attenuating upper harmonic frequencies, downsampling is removing samples that were used to capture the upper harmonic frequencies. The result is different enough that you should investigate the difference in the two sounds for advanced beat making.

ACTIVITIES CHAPTER 14

Listening

Using your favorite playback app, listen to "How to Love" by Lil Wayne (2011). Make note of the grid tuning. Would you use automatic or graphical tuning to achieve this vocal sound?

Similarly, listen to "The Rhythm of the Night" by Corona (1993) and "RITMO (Bad Boys for Life)" by J Balvin, Black Eyed Peas (2019). Can you identify the two different tempos? Would you use rhythmic, monophonic, polyphonic or varispeed TCE to achieve the difference in tempos while preserving the pitch?

When you feel that you have sufficiently analyzed these compositions, move on to the production exercises for this chapter.

Production

Access the practice files for these activities via the link and code on the first page of this book.

Additionally, you should purchase a version of "Rhythm of the Night" by Corona to experiment with time compression and expansion. Please refer to your DAW or third party plug-in manual for the use of your specific pitch tools.

Download
DAW Track 14.1 PC's How to Love

1. **Sing to the beat.** Import the stereo mix of "PC's How to Love" to your DAW. Sing the lyrics of "How to Love" recorded on a separate track.
2. **Sing to the separated files of the beat.** Import the individual files to have control over each sound. Sing the lyrics of "How to Love" on a separate track. Mix to taste.
3. **Create your own beat.** Use the virtual instruments in your DAW to create your own beat and "tuned" melody that sounds like the tuned melodies in hip-hop.

CHAPTER 15

Mixing Hip-Hop

To mix hip-hop well is to be knowledgeable about the art of mixing. Or, you can be a great listener of good mixes that communicates well with someone who is knowledgeable about the art of mixing. Mixing is an art within an art. A good mixer must understand how to service the song, the producer, the artist, and/or the record company's pre-mastered vision of what the audience will hear. The distribution of frequencies (height) from 20 Hz to 20 kHz, panorama (width) within the stereo field, levels (depth) of voltage, and other intangibles (such as reverb, delays, and file modification) related to the production team's vision for the composition are all under the control of the mixer.

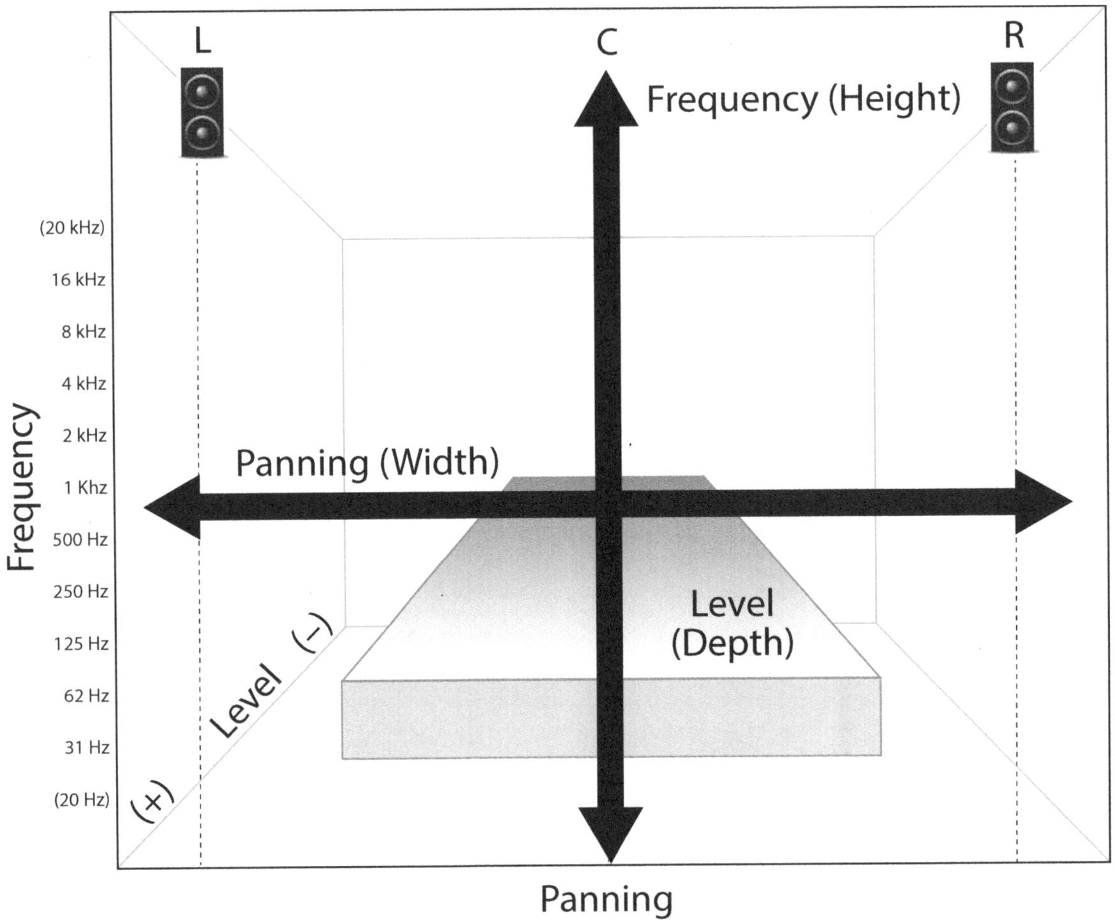

FIG. 15.1. Frequency, Panning, Level

One of my own favorite mixes is the song "One More Chance/Stay with Me (Remix)" (1995) by the Notorious B.I.G. ft. Faith Evans, produced by Rashad Smith. We mixed it at the peak of the 1990s hip-hop boom, and it contained elements that could compete in most hip-hop eras.

In that record, an underlying sample from "Stay with Me" by DeBarge (1983) was augmented with a kick drum, rim shot, snare drum, hi-hat, shaker, bell tree, finger-chimes, and bass synth in the Akai MPC3000. The composition was laid out on a large-format console and, over several days, moved between two studios. One studio had a Neve VR60 and the other had an SSL 4000-G Series. Each fader on the console represented an individual instrument, the DeBarge sample itself being one of those instruments.

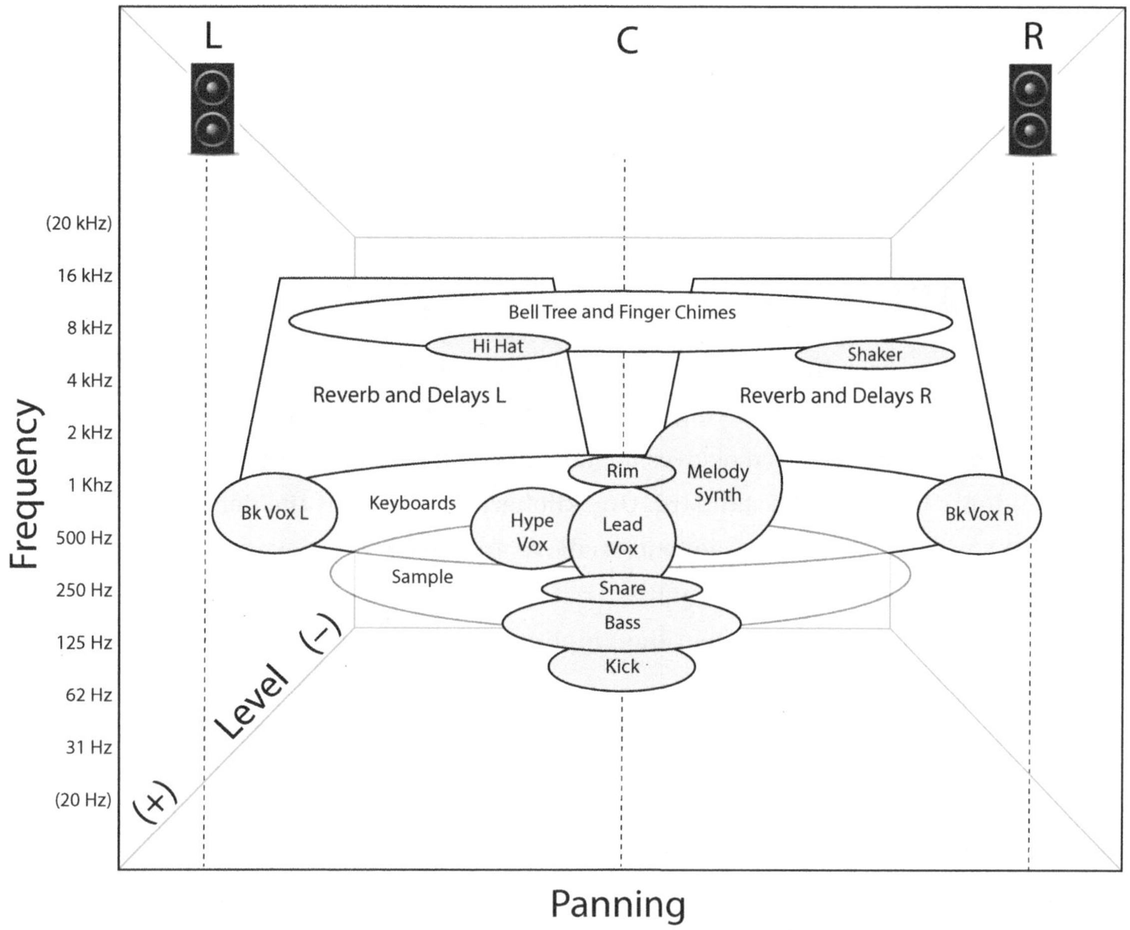

FIG. 15.2. Visualization of "One More Chance/Stay With Me (Remix)" by the Notorious B.I.G. ft. Faith Evans

Once all the audio was leveled, panned, EQ'd, and compressed, reverb and delays were added to enhance the ambience. Large-console automation was also used for mutes and a swell on the sample that happens each time the second, weaker keyboard phrase plays. I'll never forget sitting at the Neve VR console for the final mix, riding a stereo pair of faders to get a better balance between the two keyboard phrases in that sample.

Mixing has evolved, however, and the more modern approach to mixing is *in-the-box* (ITB) mixing. All of the tools that were once on the console now reside inside computers. The mix mode in most DAW software packages visually emulates analog console faders, dynamic processors, time-based processors, and routing systems. There are many debates concerning whether a pure analog path, an in-the-box path, or some hybrid of the two is better for hip-hop music production, but suffice it to say, practice does make perfect with any and all of these tools and techniques.

Mixing is a subjective art that is defined by each mixing engineer's own personal taste, skill level, or both. No two mixing engineers in hip-hop will mix the same way, and no two songs presented to those mixing engineers will pose the same set of mixing issues.

Hip-hop mixing is a creative art. The creative artists who are the mixing engineers in hip-hop solve problems that they perceive have resulted from the recording process. What I mean by "solving problems in the recording process" is not that the recording is flawed, but that the recording has captured information that needs to be enhanced, and enhancing the information is the problem that needs to be solved.

EARS/BRAIN

Where do you begin mixing? Your ears/brain! Your ability to perceive sound is the most important part of mixing a hip-hop composition. A scientific look at human perception across the ten octaves of audible sound resulted in the Equal-Loudness Contours ISO 226:2003 standard. One kilohertz (1 kHz) was the default frequency (SPL) used in that study; frequencies above and below 1 kHz were rated for equal perception. What we found out is that humans can hear some sounds louder and some sounds lower when the amplitude remains the same between all the frequencies.

If you ask a hip-hop mixer what they are listening for, they might say "I want it to feel right." But "right" is subjective. An objective concept for mixing is to first divide the audible spectrum of human hearing into octave groupings, which would look like this:

<table>
<tr><th>Frequency</th><th>Range</th></tr>
<tr><td>8 kHz–16 kHz</td><td>High Frequencies</td></tr>
<tr><td>4 kHz–8 kHz</td><td rowspan="2">High-Mid Frequencies</td></tr>
<tr><td>2 kHz–4 kHz</td></tr>
<tr><td>1 kHz–2 kHz</td><td rowspan="2">Mid Frequencies</td></tr>
<tr><td>500 Hz–1 kHz</td></tr>
<tr><td>250 Hz–500 Hz</td><td rowspan="2">Low-Mid Frequencies</td></tr>
<tr><td>125 Hz–250 Hz</td></tr>
<tr><td>62 Hz–125 Hz</td><td rowspan="2">Low Frequencies</td></tr>
<tr><td>31 Hz–62 Hz</td></tr>
</table>

Once you grasp this division of the audible spectrum of sound, your understanding of the sonic energy embedded in the recording of each instrument needs to come into play. What does that mean? You have to gauge how much each frequency, across the spectrum of human hearing, lives in each of your recorded instruments. For instance, a hi-hat might have an abundance of energy at 8 kHz, but does it also have a huge amount of energy at 31 Hz? Or a bass has an abundant amount of energy at 125 Hz, but does it have a huge amount of energy at 16 kHz?

In chapter 1, the fundamental notes of most instrument groupings were discussed. A review of those listings will tell you what the fundamental frequencies are, but will not reveal the density of the frequencies present in the recording. This is where the magic of mixing begins to take shape in hip-hop production. The hip-hop engineer must have an understanding of the fundamental frequencies (pitch), sonic density, and harmonic amplitude contained in the sounds that have been recorded. This can be done with audio analyzers, but most professionals work from honed intuition, shaped by years of listening to recorded audio.

MIXING ENVIRONMENT

Most top-level hip-hop mixing engineers still work in the control rooms of recording studios. The acoustically treated environment of the control room is meant to minimize reflections that can distort perception of fundamental frequency, sonic density, and harmonic amplitude.

Fundamental frequency is important because songs have the potential to resonate in relationship to the *tonic* note of the song. This is the note that determines the key of the song, and the key of the song is named after it. For instance, the tonic note of "Mary Had a Little Lamb" is the third note you sing. Go ahead, sing the first three notes, then sing the whole song, and you'll find out that the third note is also the last note of the song. This is the note the song wants to end on, and the note that indicates the tonal base of the song, musically known as the tonic.

Sonic density can be described simply as how thick or thin a sound feels. A simple way to understand is to hit your open hand on a table, then ball your fist and hit the same table. You will hear a thinner sound with the open hand than you will hear with the closed hand. This is a simple demonstration of what we mean by "density."

Harmonic amplitude is the level of the harmonics appearing above the fundamental frequency of any sound in your hip-hop composition. A simple way to look at this is to look at the top notes of two instruments: the human voice and the piano. The high soprano singer's note, C6, has a fundamental frequency of 1,046 Hz; we'll call it fundamental x 1 or f1. If you wanted to add or take away timbral information from this note, you would probably boost or attenuate the harmonics above that fundamental note, instead of the fundamental note itself. There would be eighteen harmonic intervals, relative to tempered tuning, whose amplitude would change the timber of your recorded C6. They would be:

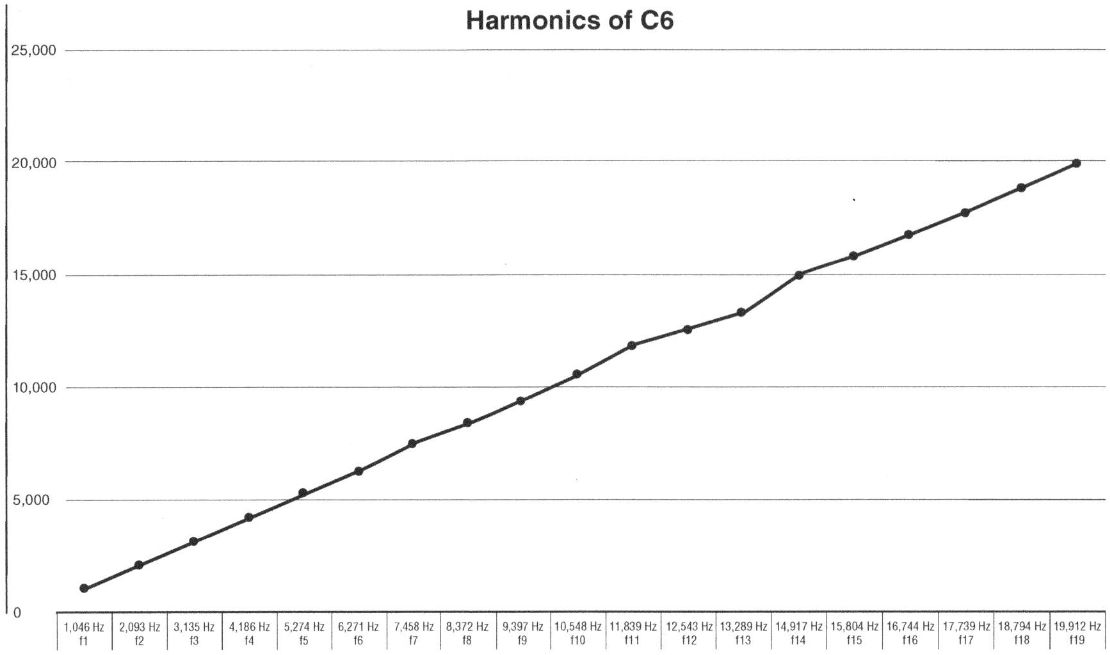

FIG. 15.3. Harmonics of C6

And on a piano's highest note (likely C8, which has a fundamental frequency of 4,186 Hz), there would only be three harmonic intervals whose amplitude would change the timber of your recorded C8. They would be:

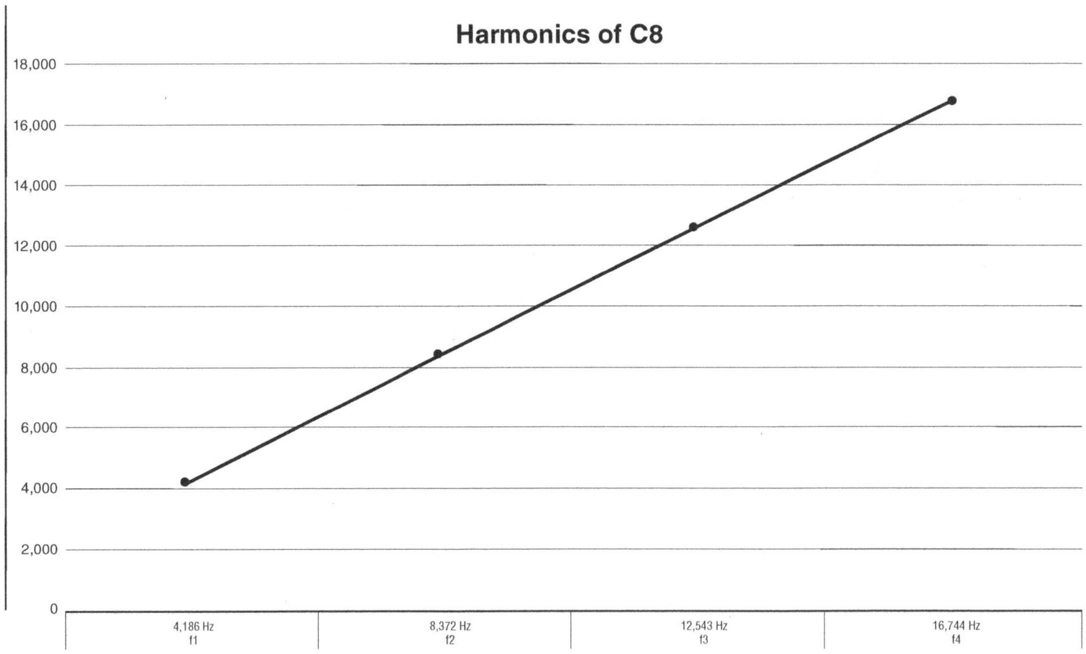

FIG. 15.4. Harmonics of C8

Improper reflections or absorptions in your mixing environment are best tamed so that your perception of fundamental frequency, sonic density, and harmonic amplitude are not distorted.

MONITORING

Our ears respond to the sound that is delivered by our playback system. So, it makes sense that the system delivering sound to our ears is the most important aspect of mixing. It is not only about EQ, compression, panning, reverb, or delays; it is also about understanding the relationship of instrument to instrument through the system delivering the audio: speakers and headphones.

With speakers, it is hard to distribute frequencies at the bottom of the audible frequency spectrum with a flat response, but easier to distribute high frequencies with a flat response. Conversely, headphones with a good, tight seal distribute a flat low-frequency response well, but a less-than-reliable flat high-frequency response. This is one reason why mixing engineers in hip-hop use multiple monitoring systems when working on a song.

A good hip-hop mix will need to sound good in a club, on car sound system, on a cheap radio, and in earbuds. A pair of ported *large monitors*, each containing one or two 15–18" transducers (or woofers), one 5–10" midrange transducer (or driver), and one 1–2.5" high-frequency transducer (or horn) should cover you for the club, and if it doesn't, you can always add in an 18" (single or dual) *subwoofer* with a crossover frequency of 120 Hz or 80 Hz to make the walls shake. By the way, the frequency response of modern hip-hop records has dropped so low (25–30 Hz) that almost all hip-hop mixers are using subs—even those who resisted subs for many years, like me.

Midfield monitors are where a lot of the critical work is done in hip-hop. A pair of these monitors can each contain one 8- to 12-inch low-frequency transducer, one 3- to 5-inch midrange transducer, and one 1-inch high-frequency transducer. Samples and vocals (as well as their upper harmonics) live in the middle of the frequency spectrum, from 500 Hz to 2 kHz, and a good pair of midfield monitors will help the focal points of the record to translate well in a car's audio system. The trick to successful monitoring is to really practice by listening and working on everything through your speakers of choice for a period of time.

My personal "weapons of choice" for mixing hip-hop compositions are *nearfield monitors*. Nearfield monitors are a pair of speakers with one 5- to 8-inch low-frequency transducers and 1- to 2-inch high-frequency transducers, per speaker, with a fixed crossover point. I still own a few pairs of Yamaha NS-10 nearfield monitors. It might seem counterintuitive to mix hip-hop on something that is inefficient in the low end, harsh in the midrange, and adequate with high frequencies, but I grew up in a generation where hip-hop mixes done on nearfield monitors created boom-box culture and eventually took over urban radio. Some hip-hop mixers go even smaller with their nearfields and use 4.5-inch driver Auratone monitors. Now these really sound like a cheap radio, but the philosophy with both the NS-10s and the Auratones is that if you can make your mix sound good on them, your mix will translate well to all other systems. The small speakers of the current generation are your computer speakers.

For most, headphone monitoring is a normal part of listening to music. It has become synonymous with the DIY (do-it-yourself) culture of DAW recording and mixing. And, in theory, any monitoring system used by the hip-hop beat maker, producer, or mix engineer consistently over a period of time should be able to yield positive results. A drawback to headphone and earbud monitoring is that they can easily deceive you because of the small drivers' close proximity to the ear canals. If headphones are your weapons of choice, practice will make perfect, and referencing your work in as many other monitoring situations outside your working environment as possible is recommended.

LEVEL

Mixing hip-hop records is all about *level*. Everything is level. Volume is overall level, panning is the level of the left and right, dynamics are level management, EQ is level management at narrow frequency bands, and time-based effects are level distributed across time.

What does that look like in your mix? Your whole record will have a level. In your DAW, a healthy level that will not distort is defined by some of the more popular streaming services as –14 LUFS (Loudness Units Relative to Full Scale, which matches how your ears actually perceive sound).

This overall level idea can be tricky because if you stay within these guidelines, and you should, your hip-hop mix will sound quiet next to mastered hip-hop compositions in the marketplace. But remember, this is mixing, not mastering. When you deliver a non-distorted mix to a mastering engineer, he/she is able to elevate the levels, usually with a more efficient handling of digital overs than on your home DAW.

PANNING

While there are some hip-hop producers who believe most of the music should be in the center so you don't miss anything if you are across the room on the other side of the club, hip-hop production at the top of the charts definitely takes advantage of the stereo field.

Pads are the first mixing consideration for width in the mix. The next parts to be considered are background vocals.

Hi-hats can move out of the center a bit, to about one o'clock if there is one hi-hat, or three o'clock if there is another hi-hat or high-end percussion instrument on the other side of the mix at nine o'clock.

The lead vocal, kick, snare, and bass will usually be centered in a hip-hop mix. Even claps and snaps will show up in the center of the stereo field, but their high frequency content gives them the flexibility to be placed in an even left, right stereo balance for some producers.

Samples and loops are treated according to the value of information in each one. A sample that is dominant on the lower end of the frequency spectrum will more likely be processed in mono, while a sample that is dominant in mid and high frequencies will have a bit more flexibility with its stereo widening possibilities.

Your recorded audio does not always have to have static panning. It can move left, center, and right across the stereo field. This type of panning can be created with panning devices or DAW automation. This type of panning can also be drawn or recorded in your DAW as automation data.

DYNAMICS

There are four main conventional types of dynamics processors: compressors, limiters, gates, and expanders. *Gates* and *expanders* were historically needed to clean up tape hiss and amp noise when we were working on analog tape, but the digital revolution yields a much quieter product. You might use a gate or an expander for creative stutters once in a great while, but other than that, everyday focus falls primarily on the compressor and the limiter.

Compressors are the most asked about—and most confusing to understand—devices I've seen young hip-hop producers and beat makers grapple with. But simply, they are automatic "turn-down" machines. Vocals and other instruments like guitars, keyboards, synthesizers, basses, horns, strings, and record samples usually benefit from a moderate leveling off by the compressor (see chapter 13, "Vocal Production"). A ratio of 3:1, with a gain reduction of not more than -6 dB, is a good way to begin using and understanding your compressor.

There are different types of compressors. The difference between them is not only the speed of compression but also the harmonic characteristics imparted by each compressor.

The *optical* compressor, like a Teletronix LA-2A, uses a light bulb (tube) to create a smooth, natural-sounding compression that is best used on vocals. The *FET* (field effect transistor) compressor, like a Urei 1176, also offers smooth characteristics that work well with vocals, even though the 1176 uses transistors to emulate the optical compressor's tube components.

The *VCA* (voltage-controlled amplifier) compressor is versatile, with a quick gain-change response, and works extremely well on transient information. The sound of hard-hitting drums on most of the hip-hop mixed in the 1990s was created using VCA compressors. SSL's G-Series console dynamics section, as well as the dbx 160X compressor, were effective at making transient instruments pop out of the mix, even at extreme 6:1 and higher ratios. Modern hip-hop mixing engineers will use the emulation characteristics of the Empirical Labs Distressor if they venture outside "the box" for mixing.

Digital technology has already surpassed analog fidelity (did I just start a war?) and as hip-hop moves further into the twenty-first century, the full gamut of analog emulations for your hip-hop final mix can be had from a wide variety of third-party manufacturers.

EQ

My EQ philosophy in hip-hop is simple but has evolved over thousands of mixes. I dial in frequencies on parametric equalizers that are relative to the tonic of the composition I am working on. Not only do I pick out the tonic frequency, but I also use the third and fifth harmonics, which happen to be the musical fifth and major third notes relative to the tonic of the composition. Using this system, I have three notes across ten octaves (thirty notes) that I can dial in for boosts or attenuations of my individual audio tracks. If you need to revisit this concept, please refer to chapter 13.

FILTERING

Filtering can take on a few different forms. There is the *low pass filter*, which is a shelf with varying attenuation slopes (-6 dB, -12 dB, -18 dB, and -24 dB). It turns down high frequencies, per octave, from a selected frequency. "Pour It Up" by Rihanna (2012) showcases this effect in the intro, middle, and end of the composition. Note: bit crushing can create a similar effect.

A *high pass filter* is a shelf with varying attenuation slopes (-6 dB, -12 dB, -18 dB, and -24 dB). It turns down low frequencies, per octave, from a selected frequency. "Lover's Ghetto" by Angie Stone (2004), produced by Rufus Blaq and me, uses this effect on the sample of "Adventures in the Land of Music" by Dynasty (1980).

A *band pass filter* shelves both low and high frequencies at varying slopes of attenuation while allowing a selected middle range of frequencies through. "The Warning" by the Notorious B.I.G. (1994) uses this effect on the vocal in bars 9–10 and 13–16 of the first verse.

Notch filtering extremely attenuates mid-range frequencies while leaving the low and high frequencies untouched. This is a great corrective tool that removes unwanted mid-range energy from an overly busy sample. "Loyalty" by Kendrick Lamar ft. Rihanna (2017) applies this technique to the vocal sample from "24K Magic" by Bruno Mars (2016).

TIME-BASED EFFECTS

For me, reverb, delay, flanging, phasing, and chorusing are the primary devices that fall under the heading of time-based effects.

Reverb (reverberation) is hundreds of diffuse delays that create ambience. All hip-hop uses reverb on vocals, but the amount varies from producer to producer and song to song. *Halls* (long 2 to 4 s reverb time), *plates* (medium .750 to 2 s reverb time), and *rooms* (short 100 ms to 1 s reverb time) are the most common reverb types you'll find in hip-hop compositions. Contrast the long, dark hall reverb on the vocal in "Unforgettable" by French Montana ft. Swae Lee (2017) with the short, thin plate reverb in "Humble" by Kendrick Lamar (2017). The treatment on Kendrick's vocal is more in line with helping the articulation of the vocalist. The long and thick vocal reverb like that used on "Unforgettable" is outside the norm of medium and thin plate reverbs used by the majority of hip-hop producers.

Delays are the bread and butter of "top of the chart" hip-hop record making. Some delays are loud in the mix and others are subtle, helping to fill out the ambience of the composition. Delays are calculated in milliseconds relative to the tempo of the composition; the formula to find the number of milliseconds per beat at any tempo is 60,000 ms/bpm = a quarter note in milliseconds. A simple *mono delay* panned to the center can add interest to a hip-hop composition. "Loyalty" By Kendrick Lamar ft. Rihanna (2017) uses a simple mono delay on the female vocal in the choruses of this composition, on the word "loyalty."

A *stereo delay* will have a few milliseconds of difference between the left and right signal, which creates a widening effect spread across the record, and a *ping-pong delay* can occur on the right, then move rhythmically to the left, back to the right, and back to the left again. You can hear a stereo delay on the vocal and a ping-pong delay on the keyboard in "XO Tour Llif3" by Lil Uzi Vert (2017).

Delays that move from left to right are called *ping-pong delays* because the first and second delays are set up as multiples of rhythmic divisions, if you want the ping-pong to sound musical. So, an eighth note on the left would be followed by a quarter note on the right, which gives the effect its rhythmic and unique name. This is actually achieved by sending an audio signal to a delay unit panned to the right that is set for an eighth note. Then that delay unit sends a signal to a delay unit panned to the left that is also set to an eighth note. The second delay unit is heard a quarter note later than the original audio signal. The second unit can now send signal back to the first unit, which will be heard a dotted quarter later and set up a loop that can go back and forth continually, or be adjusted to fade based on the level being sent from the first delay.

The *flanger* and *phaser* are periodic modulations of the delay time that sweep up and down the frequency spectrum at resonant frequencies. The flanger is a long sweep, the phaser is a short sweep. You can hear a panning flange on the word "love" at the beginning of the second verse in "Drunk in Love" by Beyoncé (2013).

A *chorus* device uses slight modulations in pitch to create a thicker sound for your instruments or vocals. This concept is used on almost all synthesizers in hip-hop, at the production level well before the mix.

That is your mixing template. Every song that has been successful in hip-hop uses the simple elements outlined in this chapter. Your job is to listen, investigate, create, listen some more, investigate some more, create some more, wash, rinse, dry, set, and repeat again. That is how everyone at the top of the charts got good.

ACTIVITIES CHAPTER 15

The best way to mix well is to listen well. Listening well means allowing yourself to be open to old as well as new ideas in hip-hop record production. The levels, panning, EQ, dynamics processing, time-based effects, and file modification are always in fascinating flux, so never stop listening and enjoying how hip-hop producers continue to expand the skill set.

Listening

Using your favorite playback app, listen to the top ten hip hop songs each week. What are the similarities and differences between these compositions (tempo, key, instrumentation, panning, reverb, etc.)? Listen for instruments that never leave, and instruments that enter and leave. Are the tempos all in the same range or is there a large variation. How many instruments are playing at any one time? When you feel that you have sufficiently analyzed these compositions, move on to the audio exercise for this chapter.

Production

Create your own:

1. Use the virtual instruments in your DAW to create your own beat.
2. Record rapping and/or singing to another track in the session with your beat.
3. Use the tuning tools from your DAW or from a third party manufacturer to make sure your rap/singing is in tune.
4. Edit all the audio in your composition until the timing and pitch of each performance sounds commercially competitive.
5. Mix the levels, panning, EQ, dynamics processing, time-based processing, and file modification over and over using processing techniques from this chapter until your original composition sounds like it can stand next to most commercially released hip-hop compositions. When you are done, start the process all over again. Continue in this creative fashion for the rest of your life, and I guarantee that you will discover your version of a hip-hop producer that is *inside the beats*.

FINAL WORDS

To be an effective hip-hop producer, you need to be proficient in one or all of the aforementioned fundamental ways to make hip-hop music . . . excessively. There is also no substitute for listening to compositions that have been successful, both commercially and critically, in order to get a sense of what makes a great hip-hop beat connect to an audience.

The compositions that were chosen for this book underscore shifts in hip-hop production throughout time. Use these as an entry to hip-hop production, but expand on them and create your own lists once you become familiar with the core principles of various styles of hip-hop.

Continue listening to current successful and critically acclaimed compositions in order to stay on top and slightly ahead of the fast-paced world of music production in general, and of hip-hop more specifically. And remember, there is no substitute for hard work.

—Prince Charles Alexander

INDEX

T

U

V

W

Y

ABOUT THE AUTHOR

Prince Charles Alexander is a multiple Grammy winning musician, recording artist, record producer, audio engineer, and professor in the Music Production and Engineering Department at Berklee College of Music where he created the minor in Commercial Record Production. He authored the graduate level Commercial Vocal Production course and co-authored the undergraduate level Vocal Production course for Berklee Online. Professor Alexander commuted for eight years between Berklee and NYU's Clive Davis Institute of Recorded Music creating and teaching innovative new courses in music production, audio engineering, hip-hop and remixing. He authored and teaches Massively Open Online Courses (MOOC's) with EdX.org and Coursera.org., has lectured at the City College of New York, Pace University, the School of Audio Engineering, the University of Oslo (Sweden), the International College of Music in Kuala Lumpur (Malaysia), the Cape Town Academy at Stellenbosch University (South Africa), and many other academic institutions around the world.

Prince Charles began his recorded music career as the producer, songwriter, lead singer, rapper and Lyricon player (a wind synthesizer) of the funk group Prince Charles and the City Beat Band. Aided by his mentor Maurice Starr (the producer of New Edition and New Kids on the Block), and his business partner Tony Rose, he secured record deals with Greyhound, ROIR, Virgin, Atlantic, and Unidisc before disbanding his group and focusing on music production and audio engineering.

As a producer and audio/mixing engineer, Professor Alexander has garnered a Best Rap Album Grammy win for *No Way Out* by Puff Daddy & The Family (1998), a Best Traditional R&B Performance Grammy win for "Wonderful" by Aretha Franklin (2004), a Best Contemporary R&B Gospel Album Grammy win for *Again* by Donnie McClurkin (2004), seven Grammy nominations, more than forty platinum and gold certifications by the RIAA (Recording Industry Association of America), and a Victoires de la Musique (a French Grammy equivalent) for his co-production of the iconic French hip-hop album *L'Ecole du Micro D'Argent*. His client list includes Mary J. Blige, the Notorious B.I.G., J Lo, Diddy, the Lox, 112, Total, Black Rob, Carl Thomas, Mase, Destiny's Child, X-Clan, Aretha Franklin, Luther Vandross, and Sting.

Prince Charles Alexander speaks annually at local Boston high schools and grammar schools, and is the subject of music production and audio engineering video interviews created by Sennheiser and Izotope. He is a member of the Producers and Engineers Wing of the Grammy Committee Board of Governors, the Audio Engineering Society (AES) and the Musician's Union Local 802 in NYC as well as managing up and coming talent through his production company Ark Angel Music, Inc. Plans to release new music as an artist are in the works as well as film projects and, of course, more books.